THESE WiNGS BELONG TO:

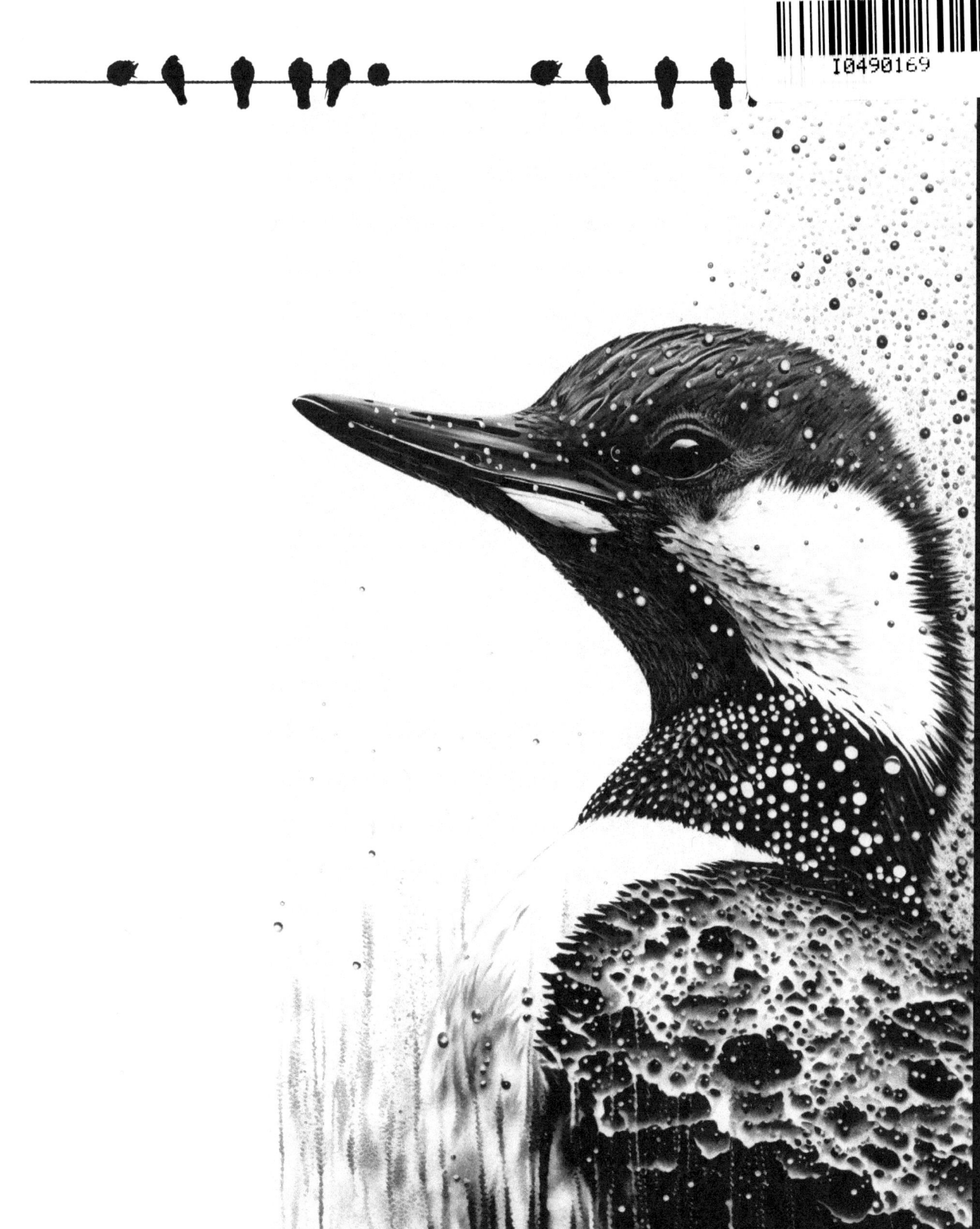

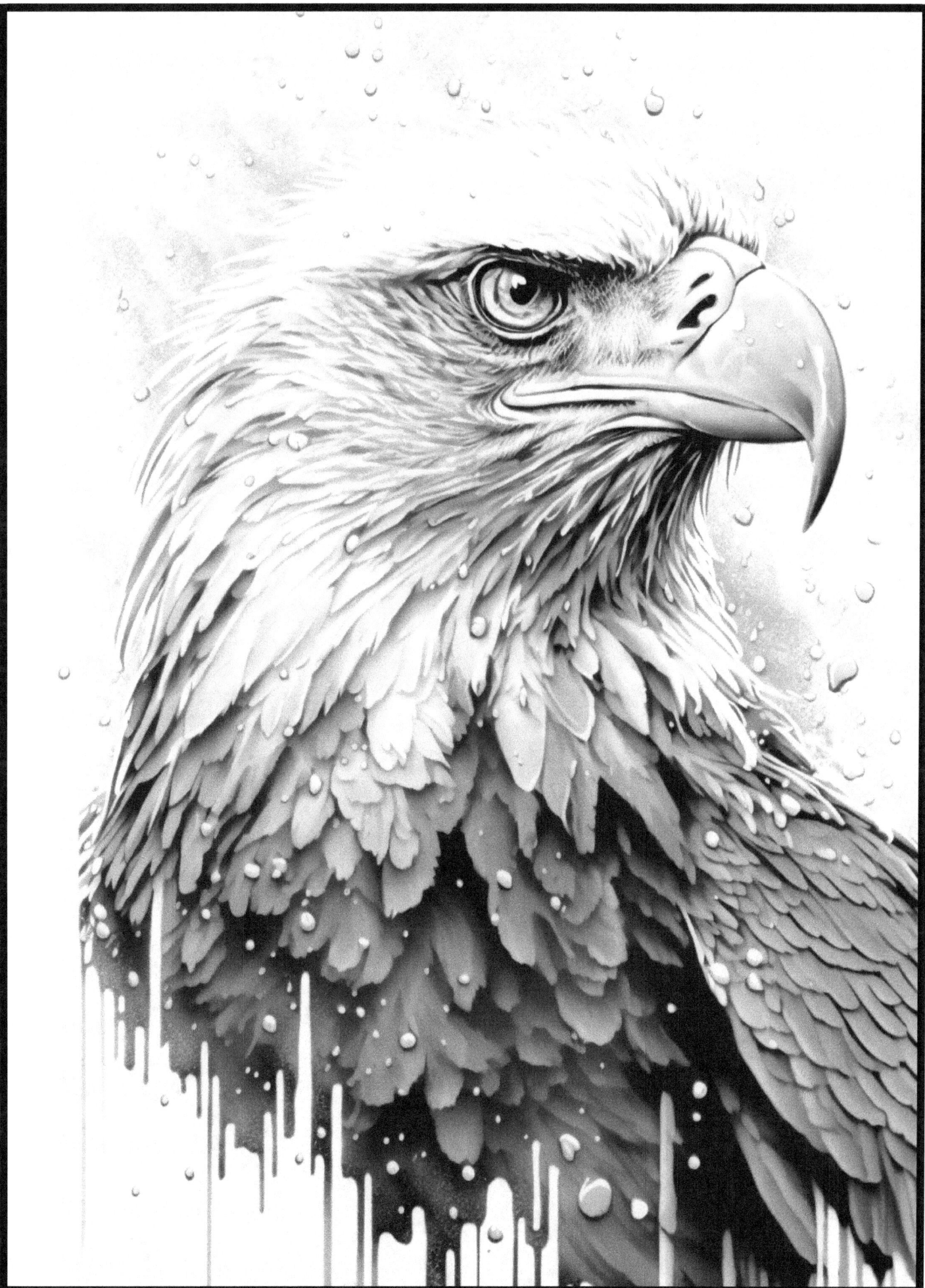

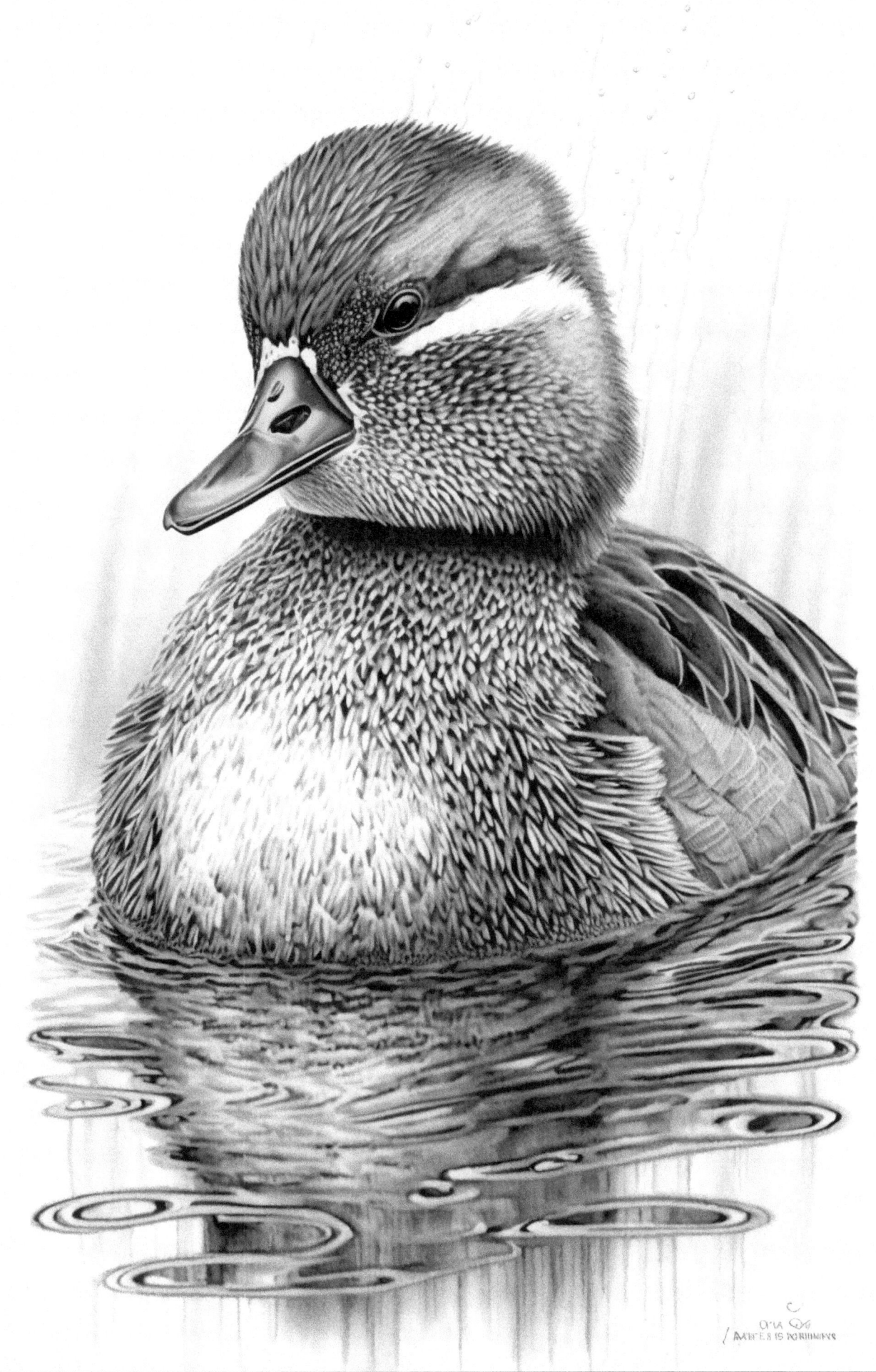

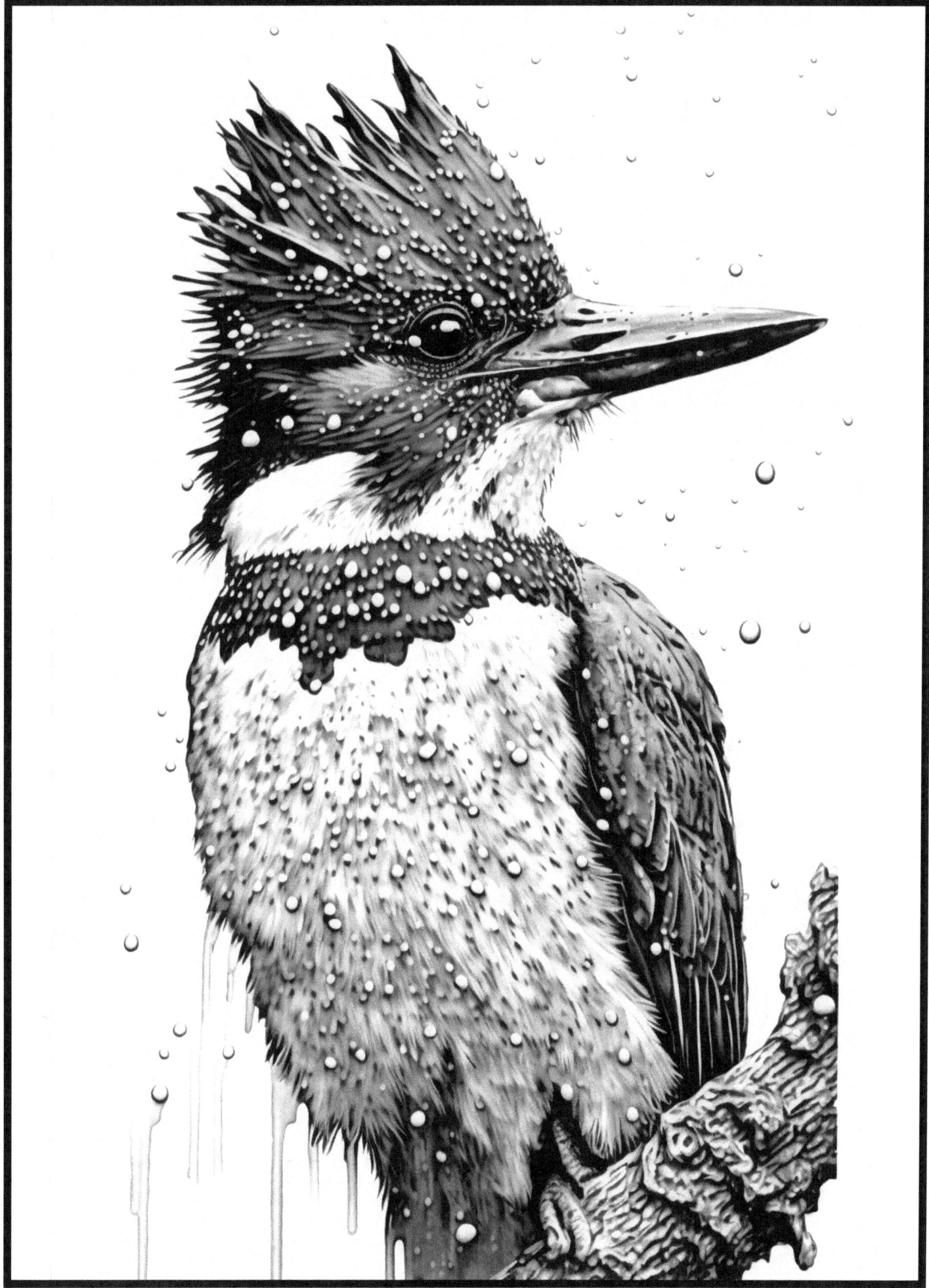

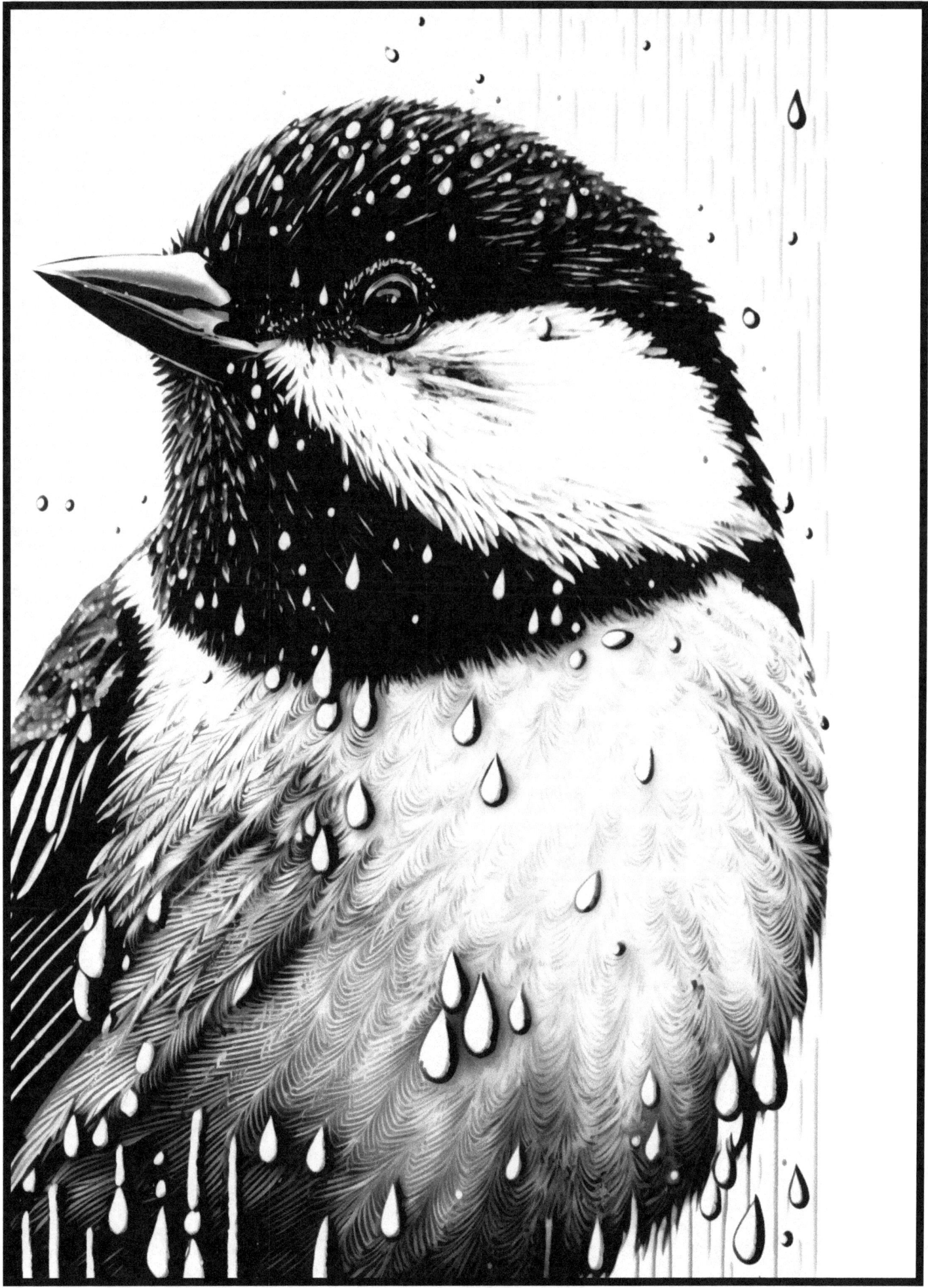

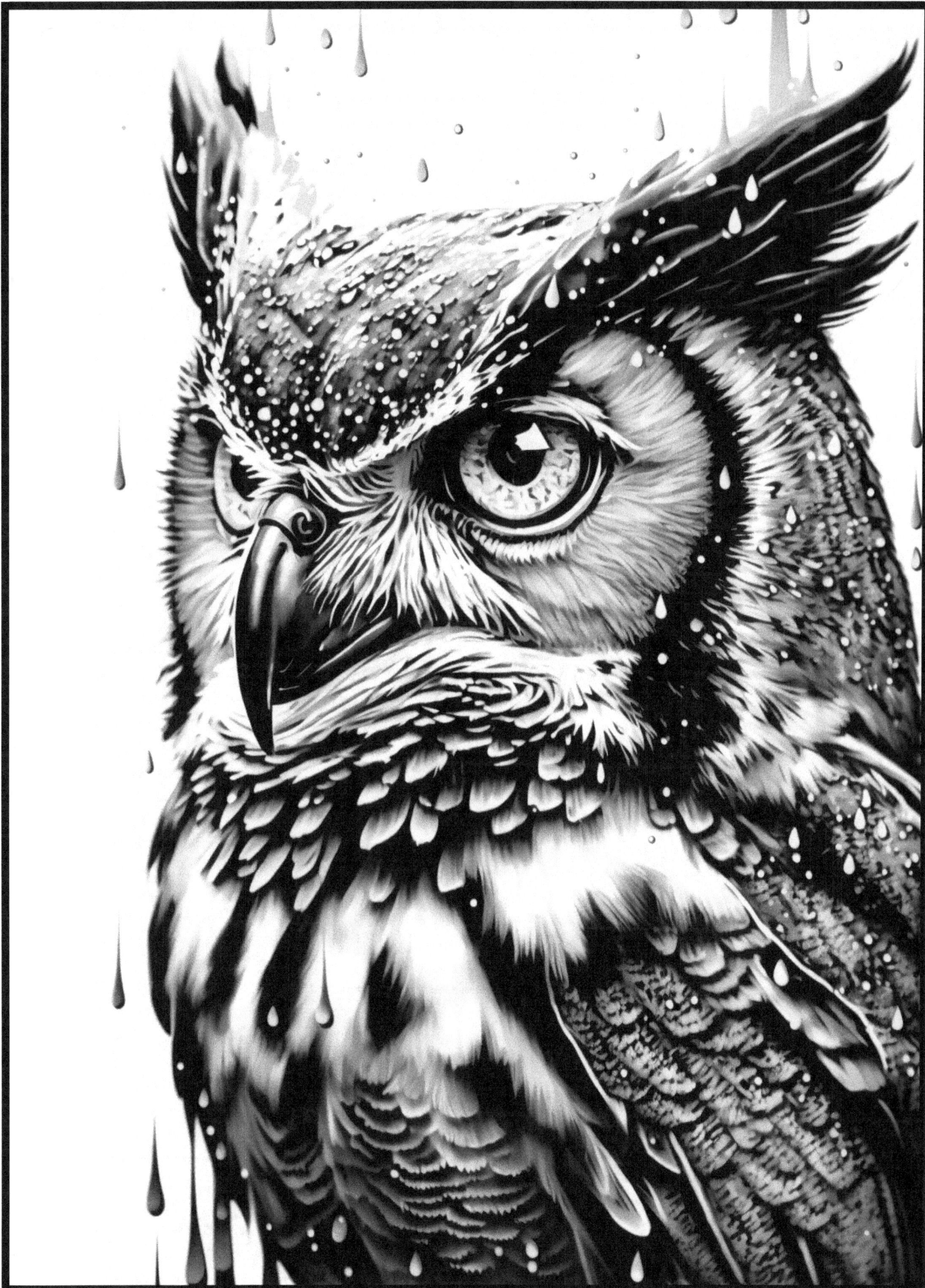

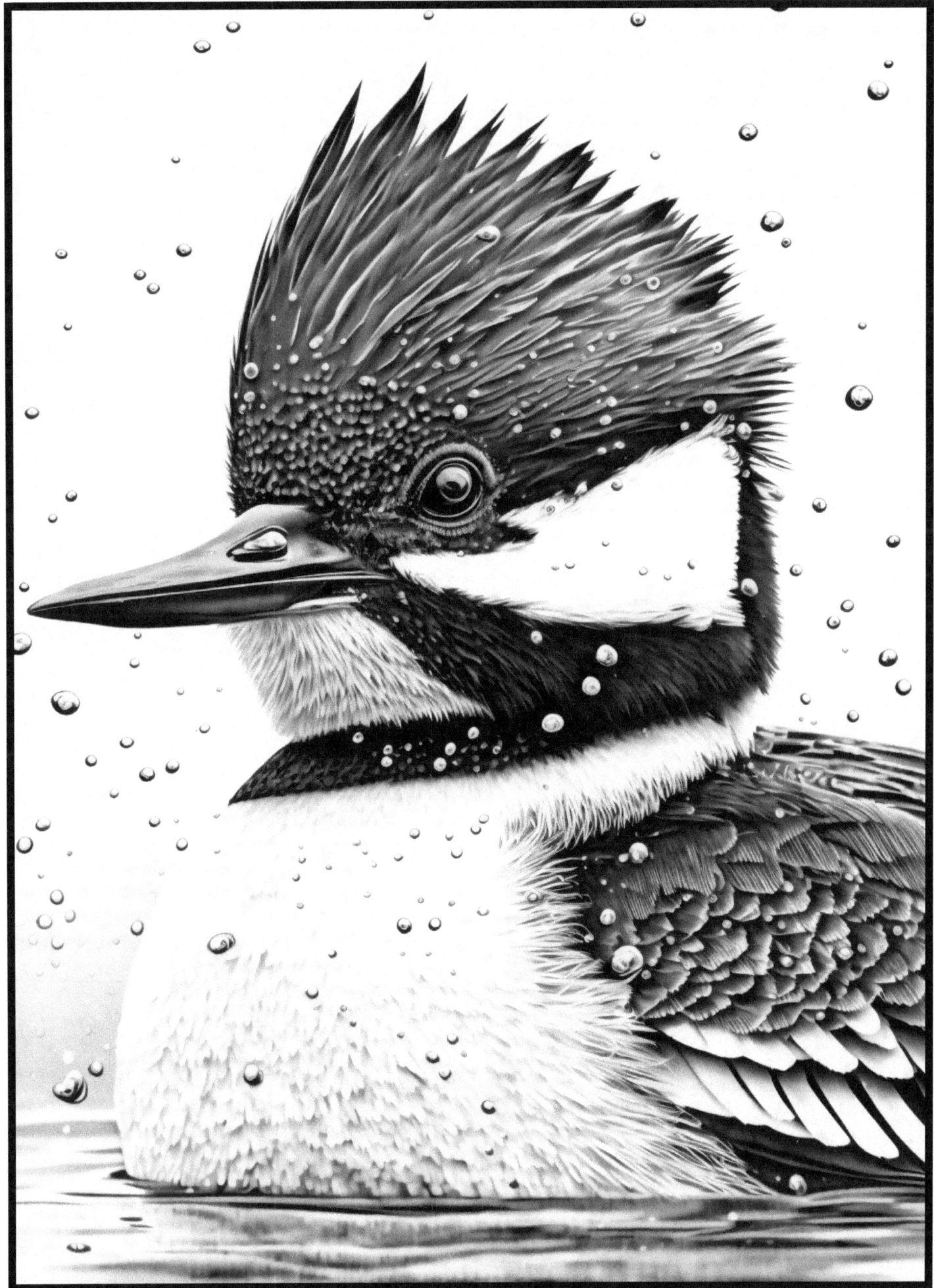

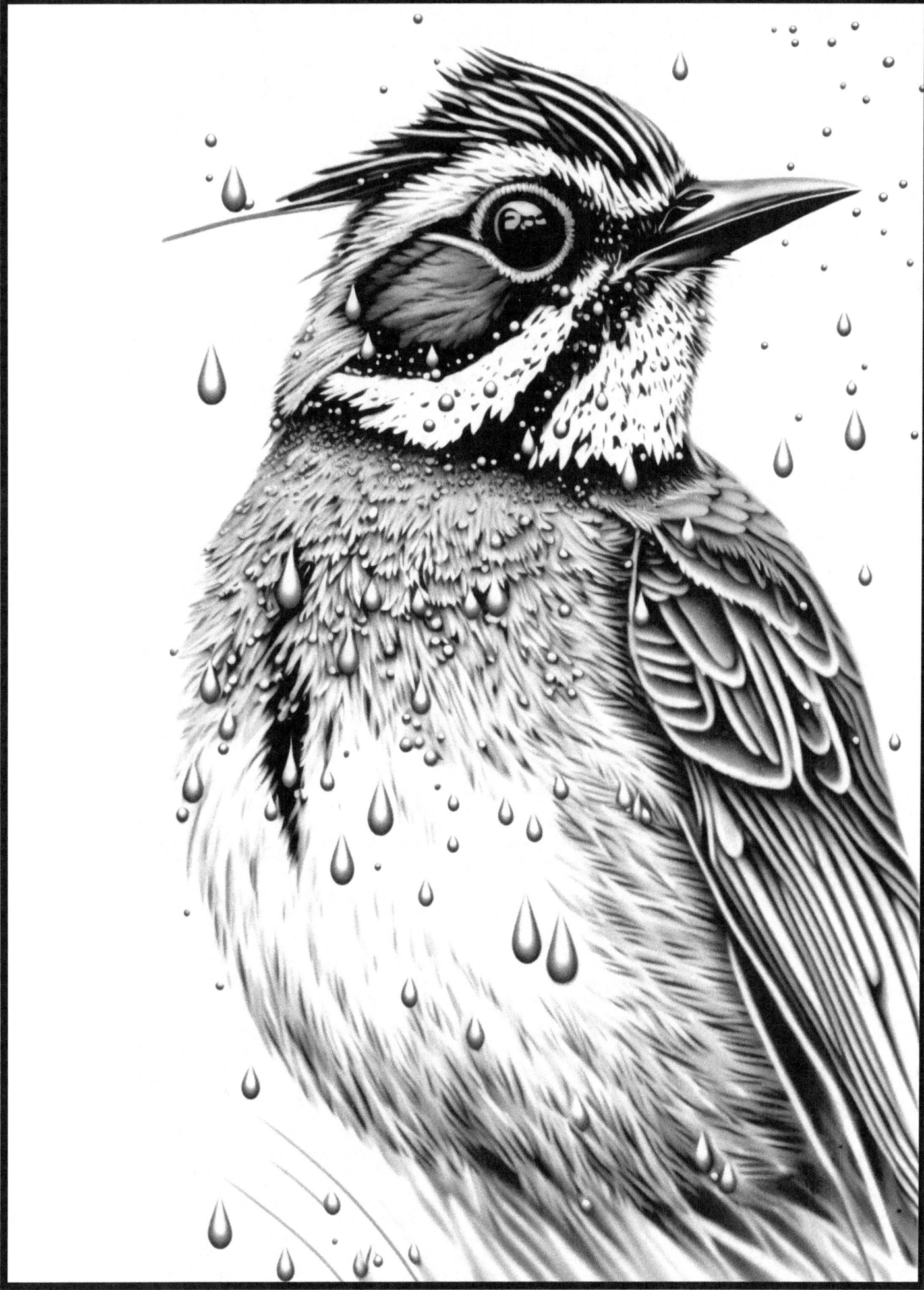

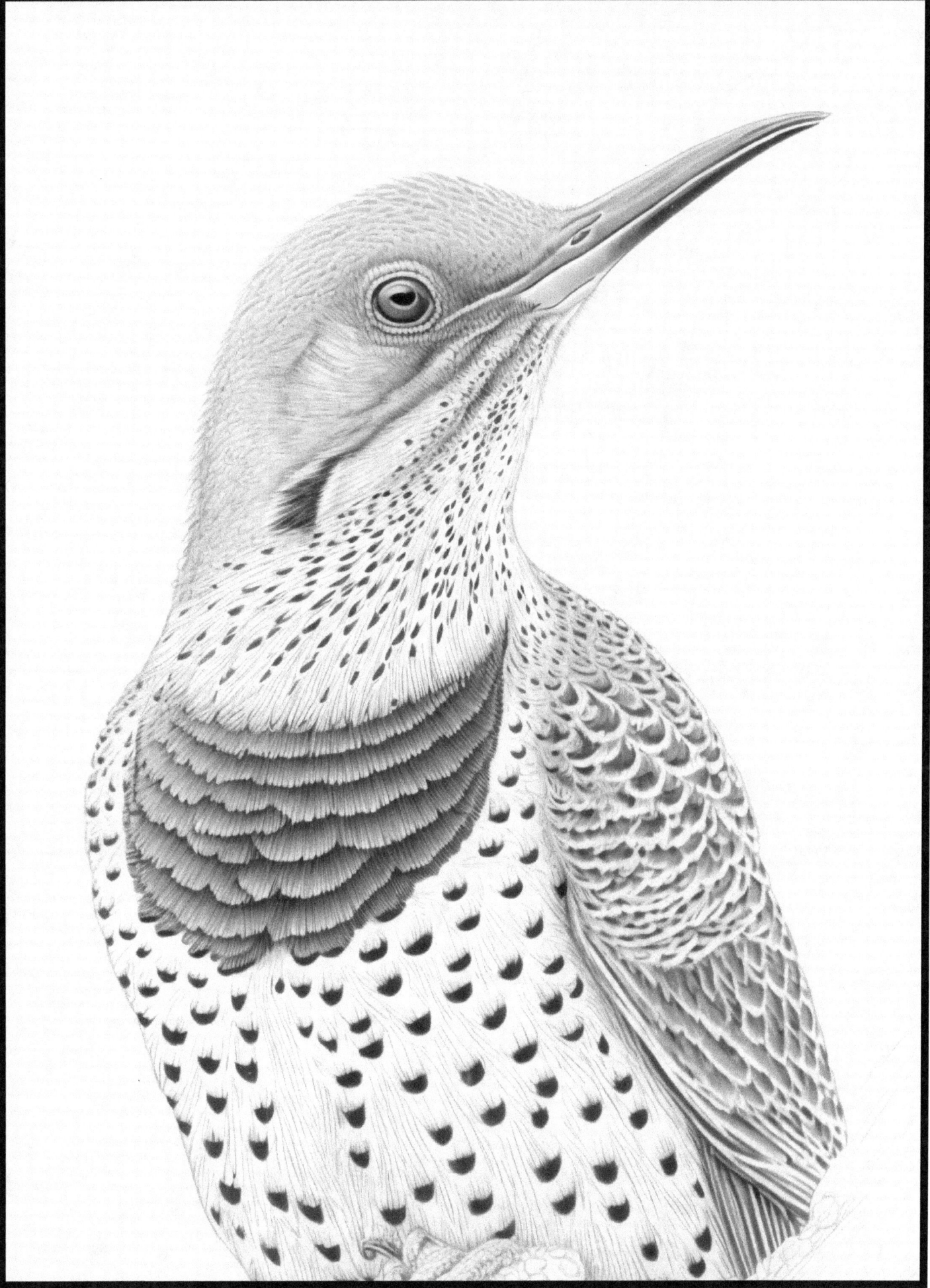

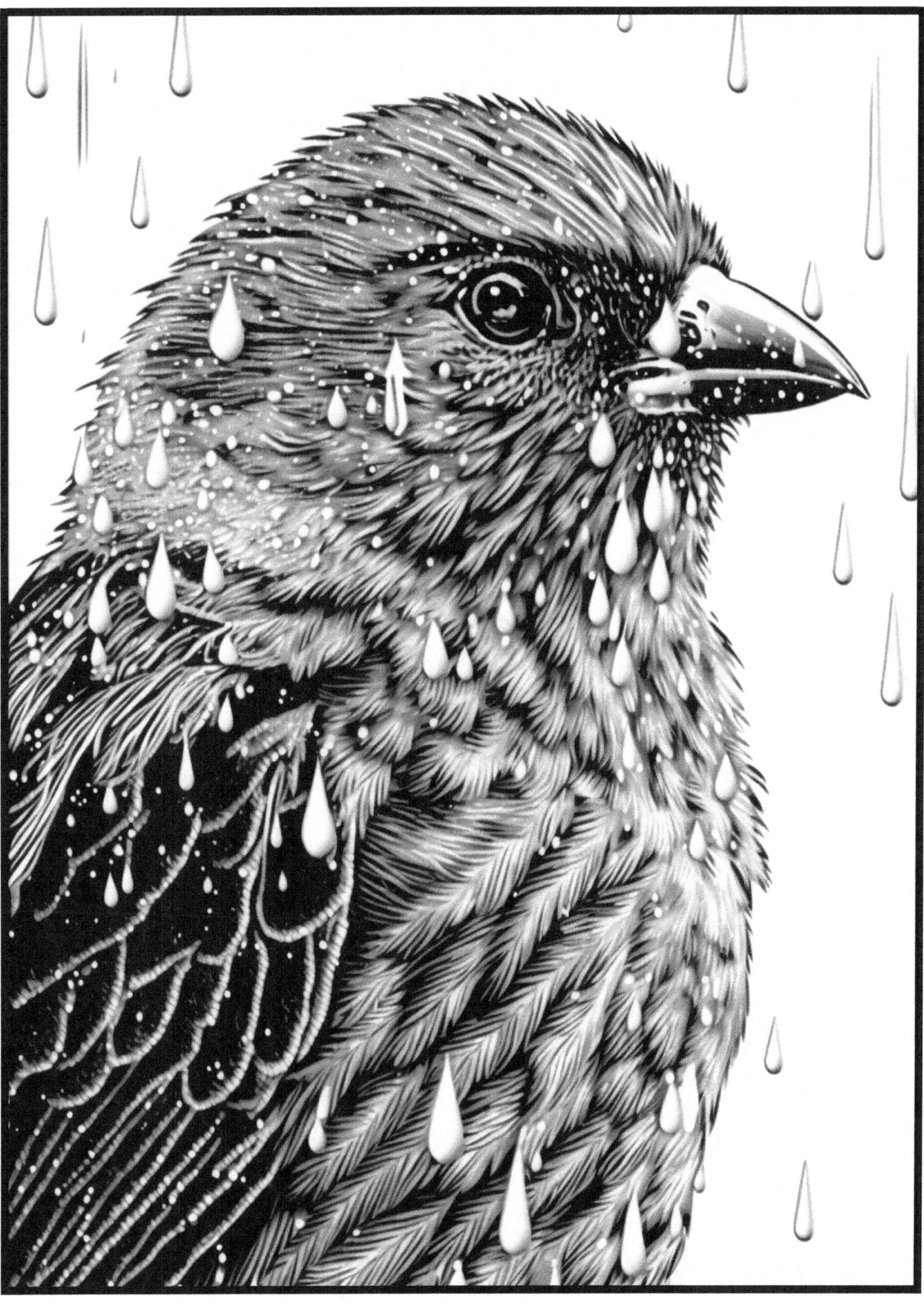

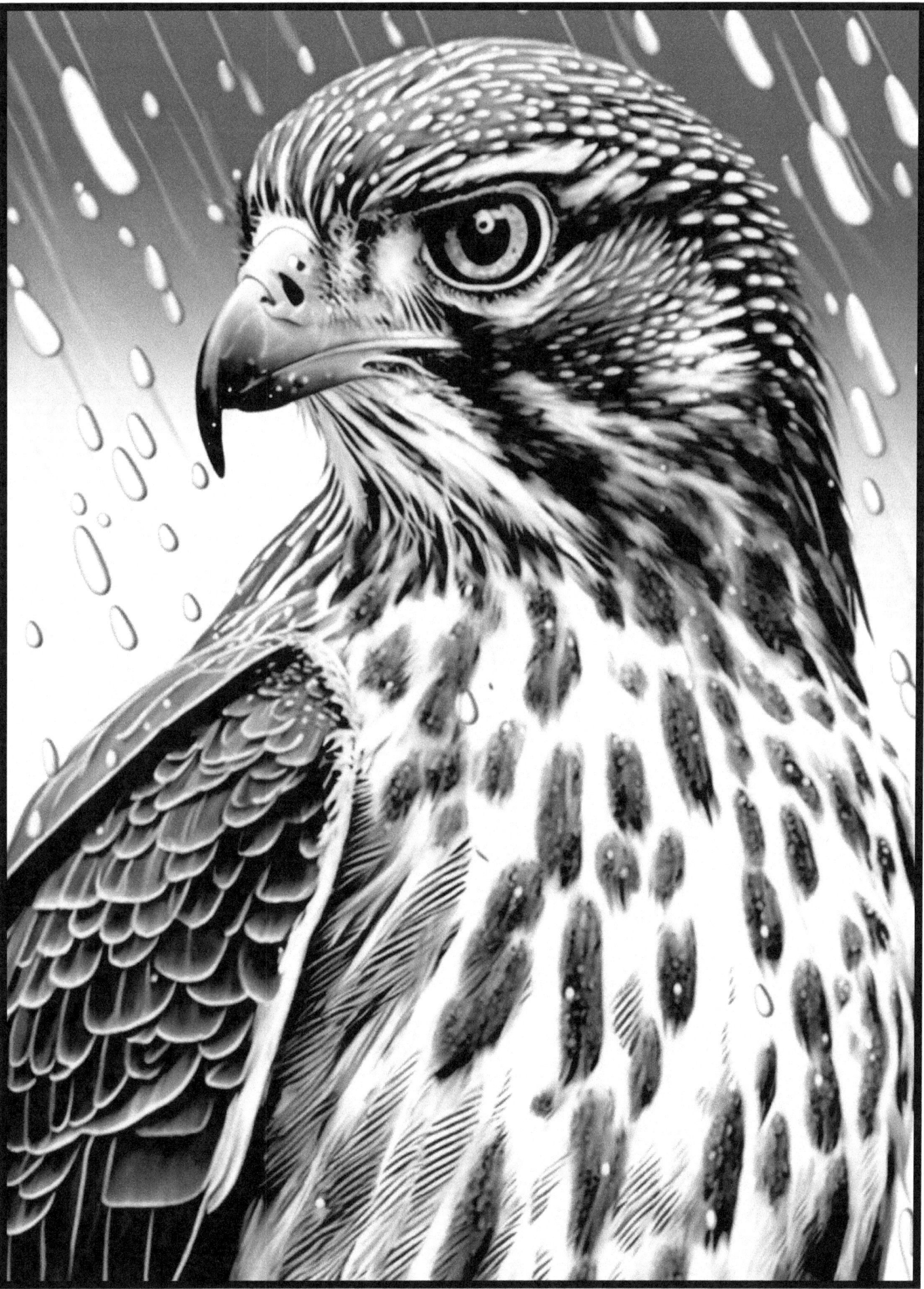

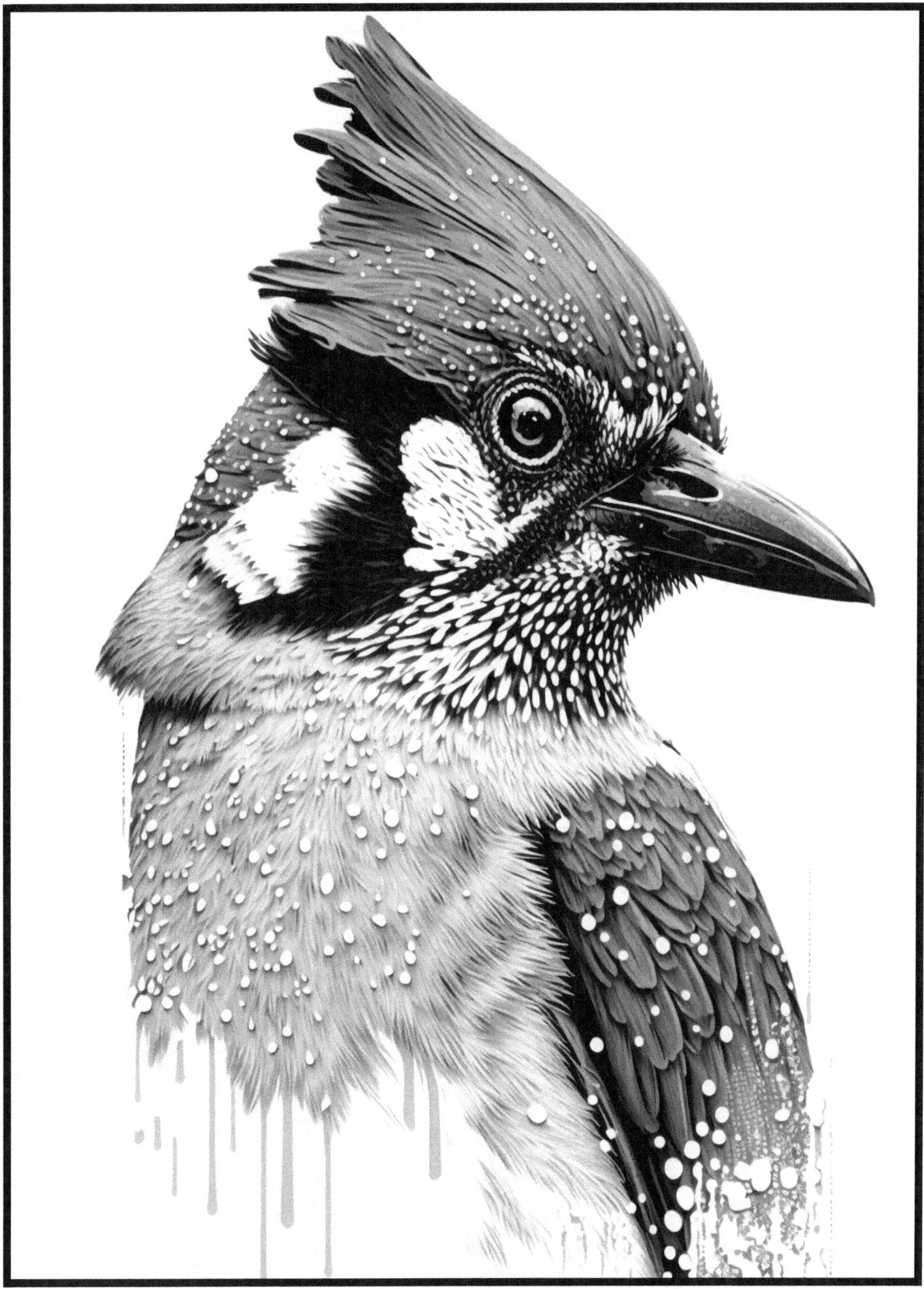

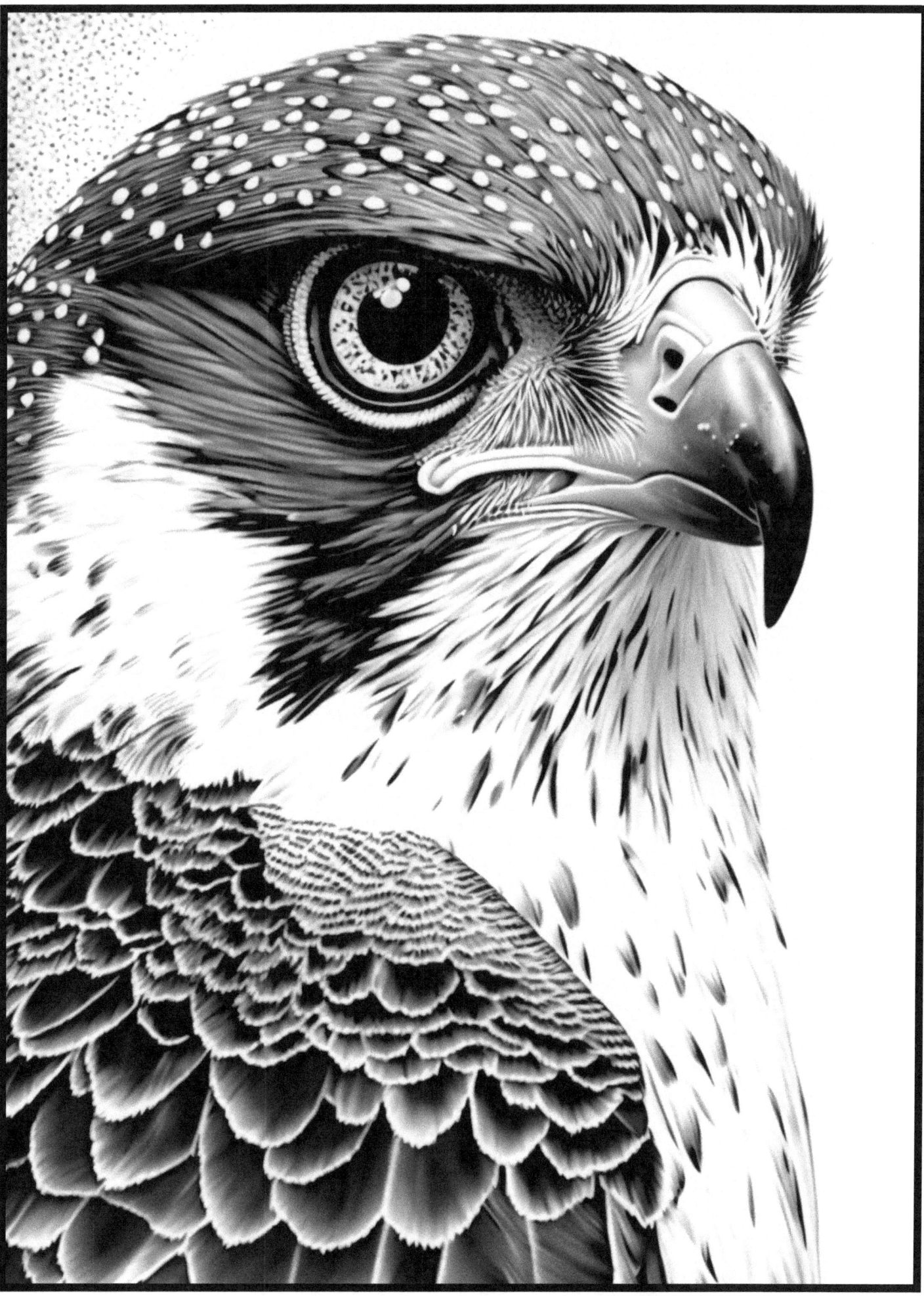

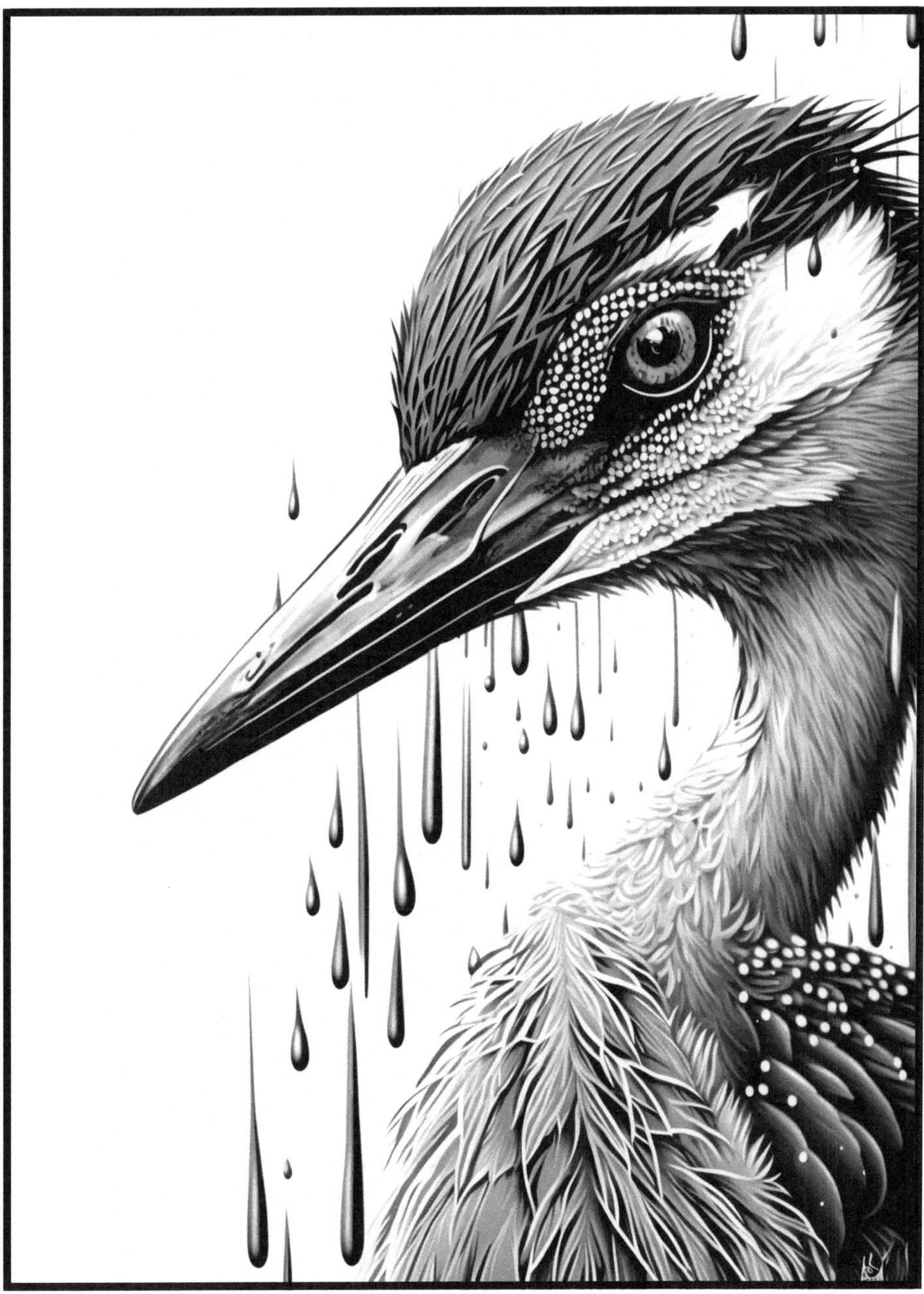

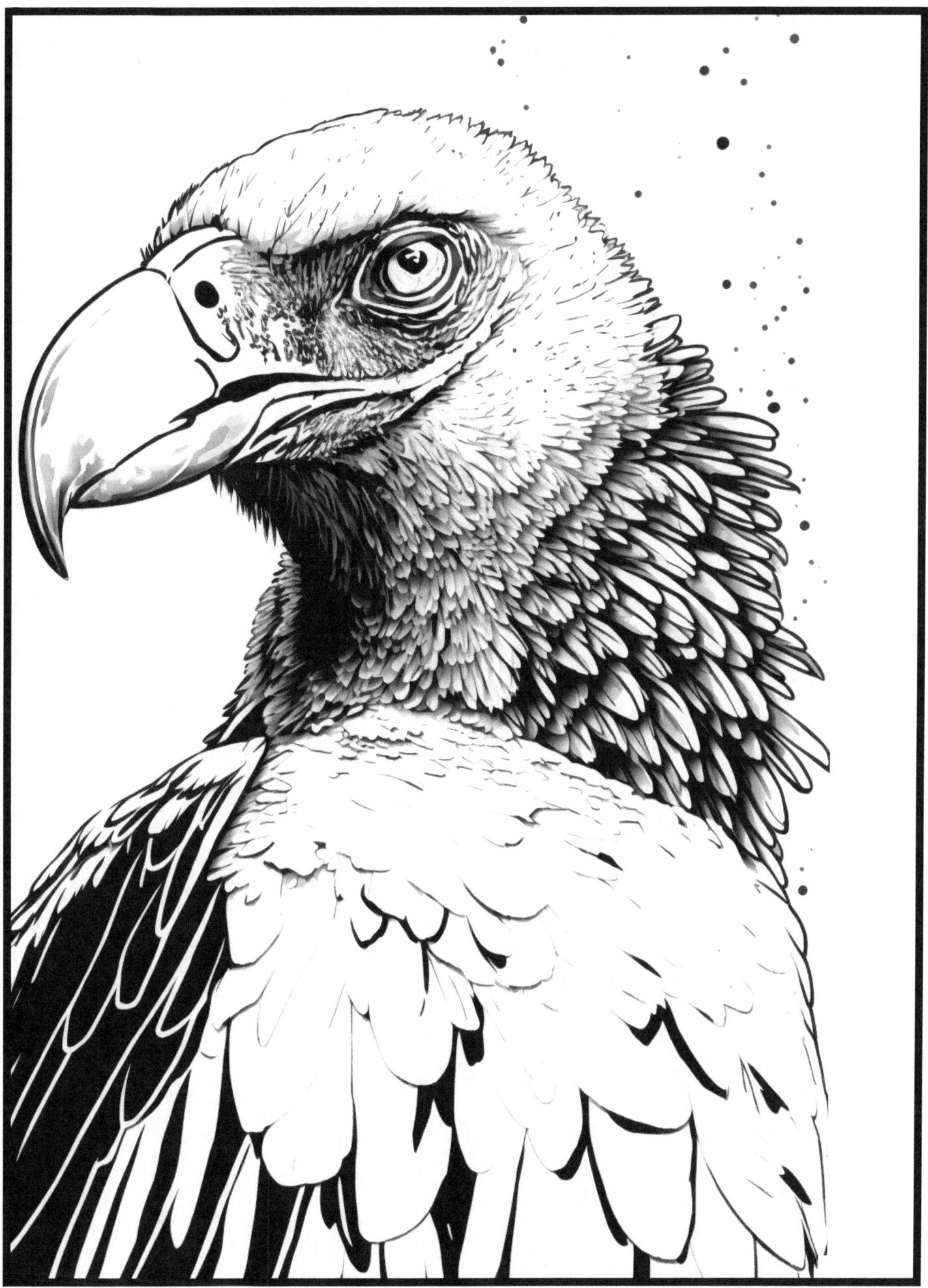

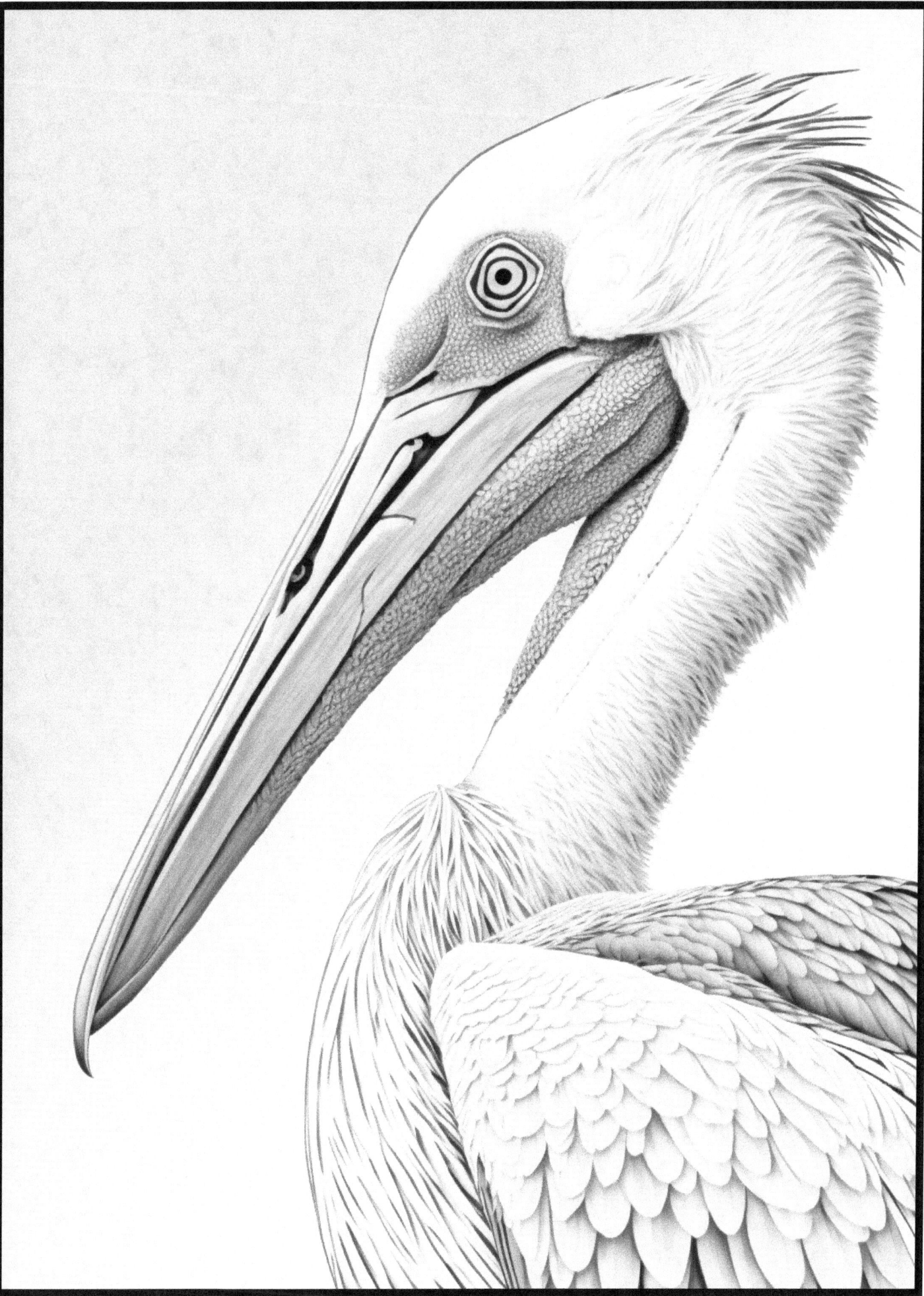

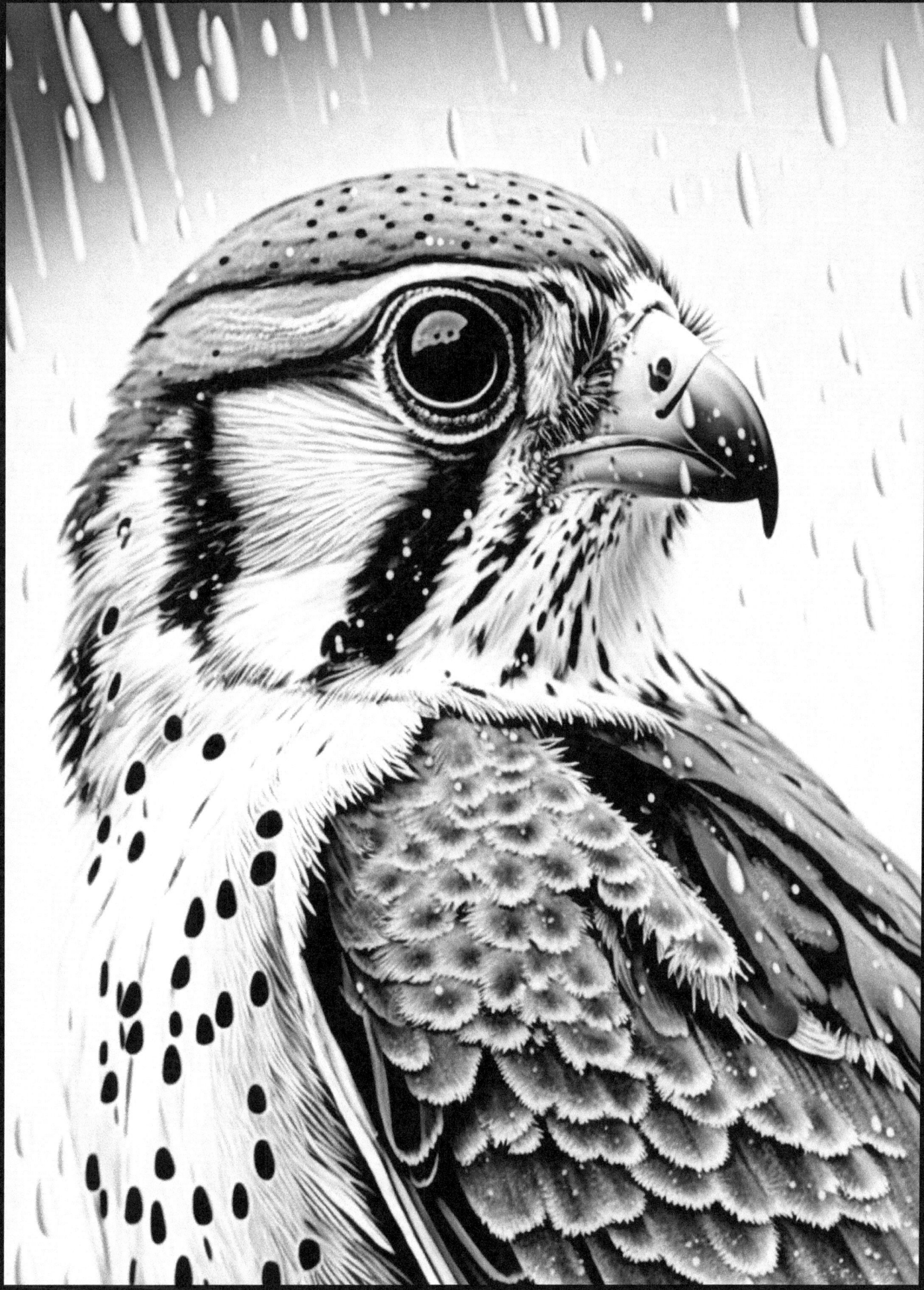

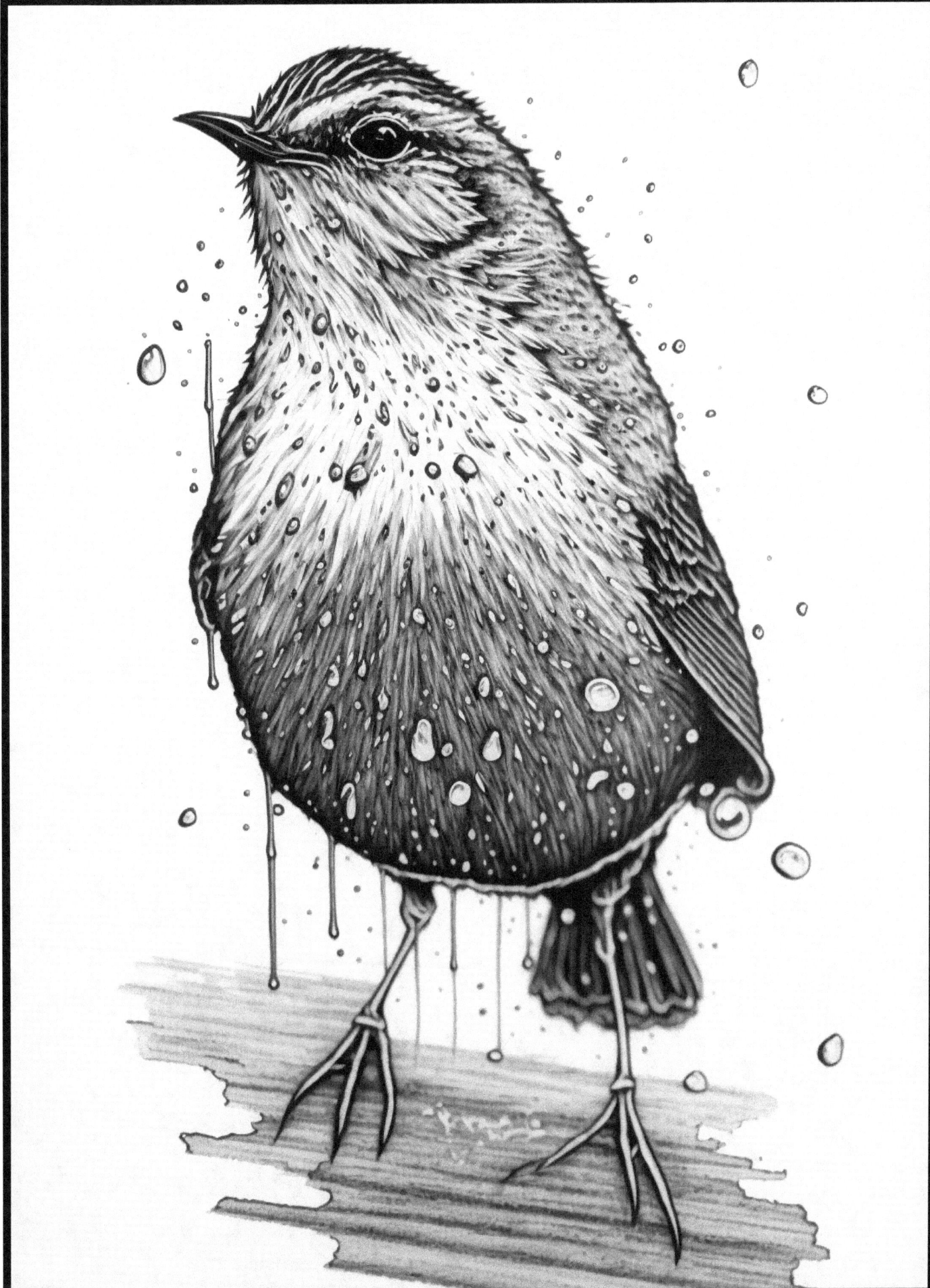

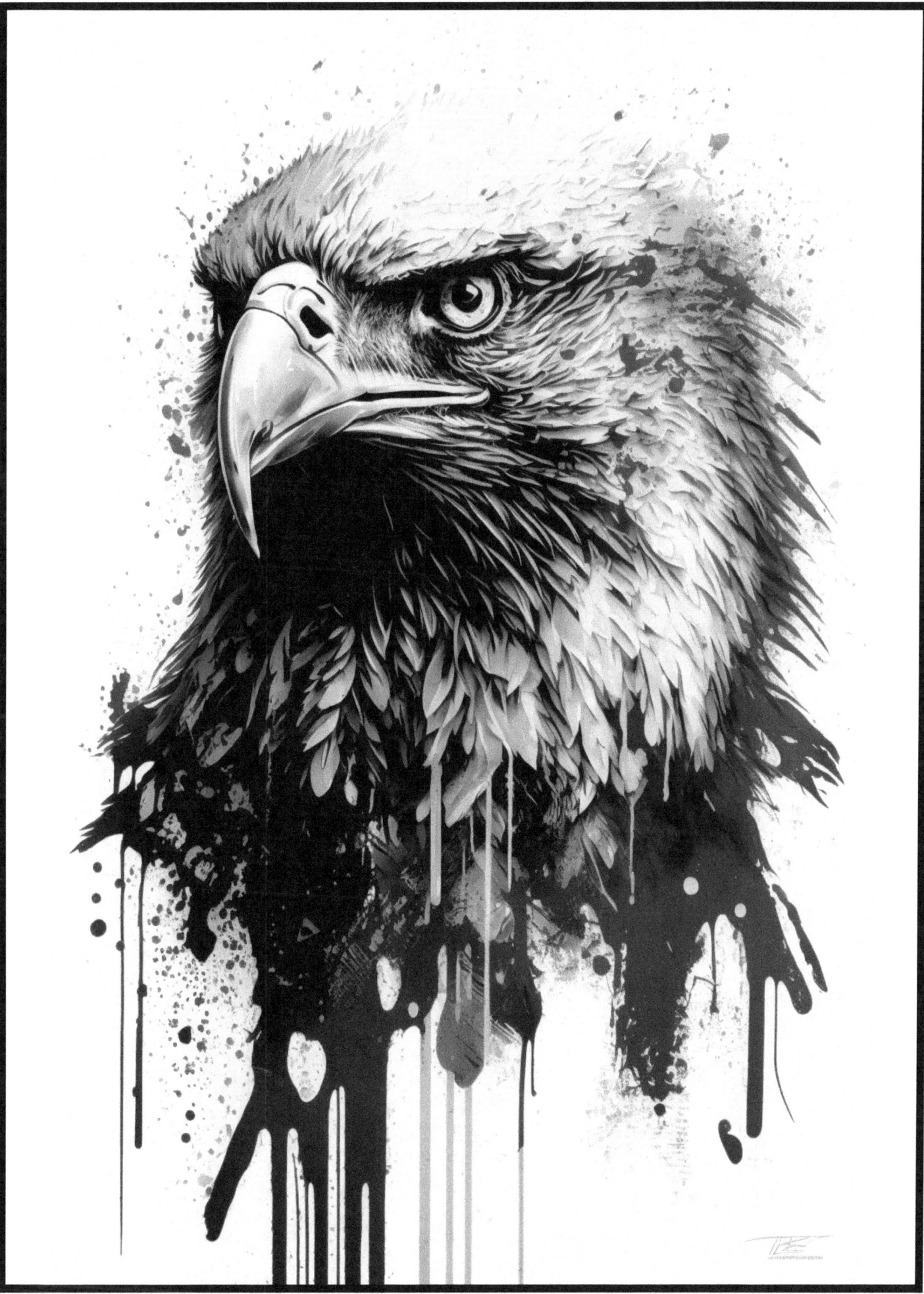

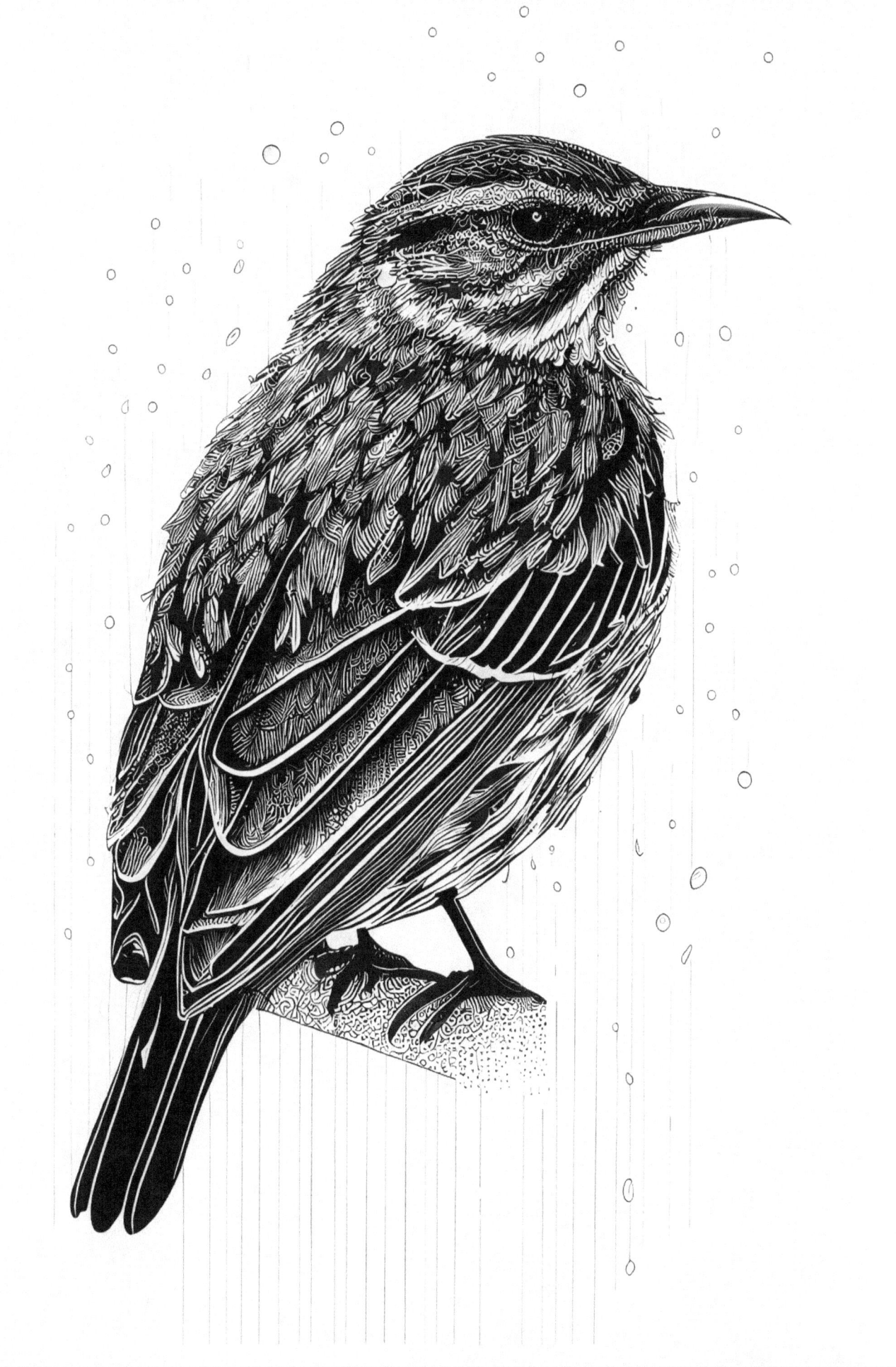

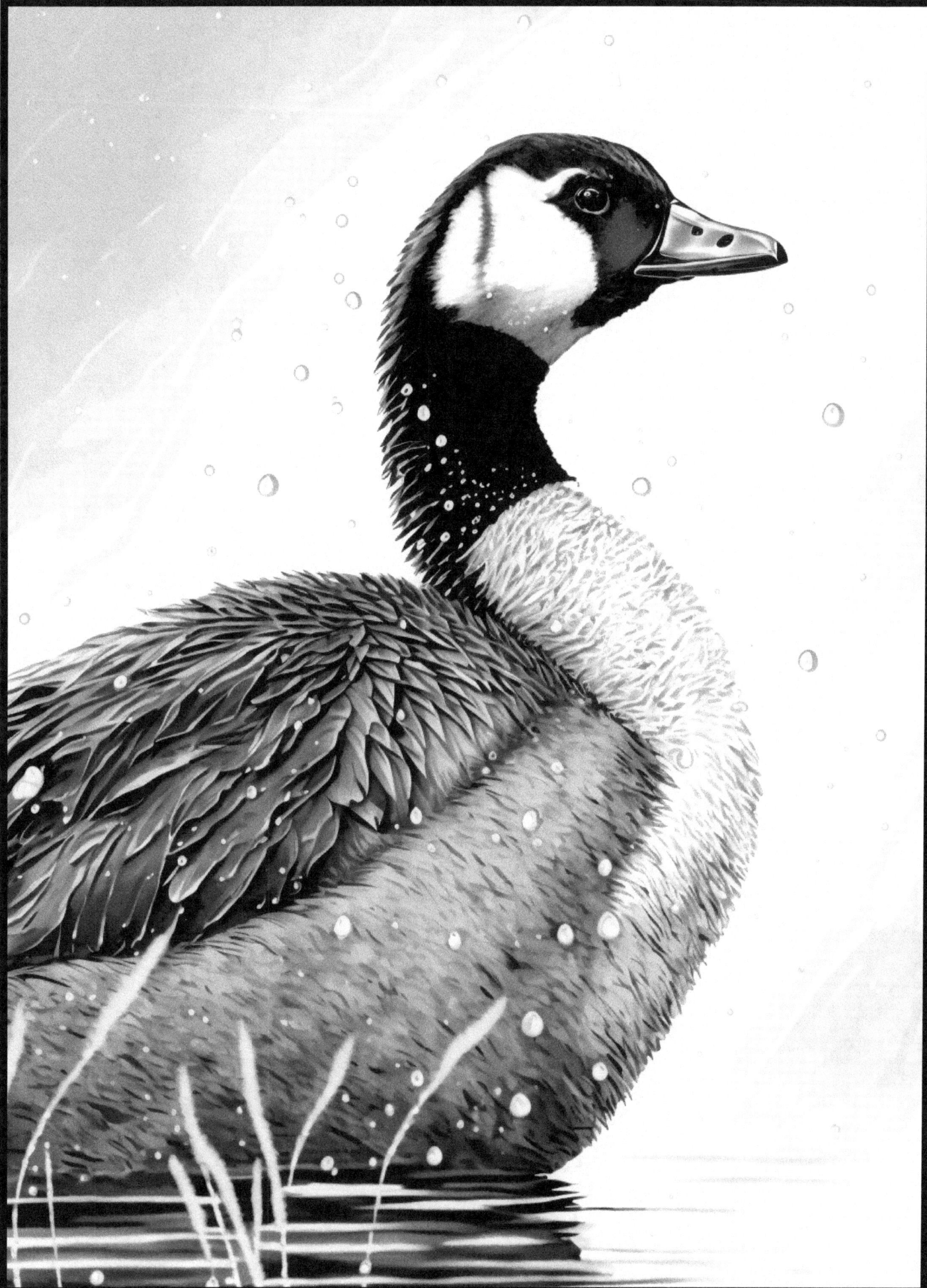

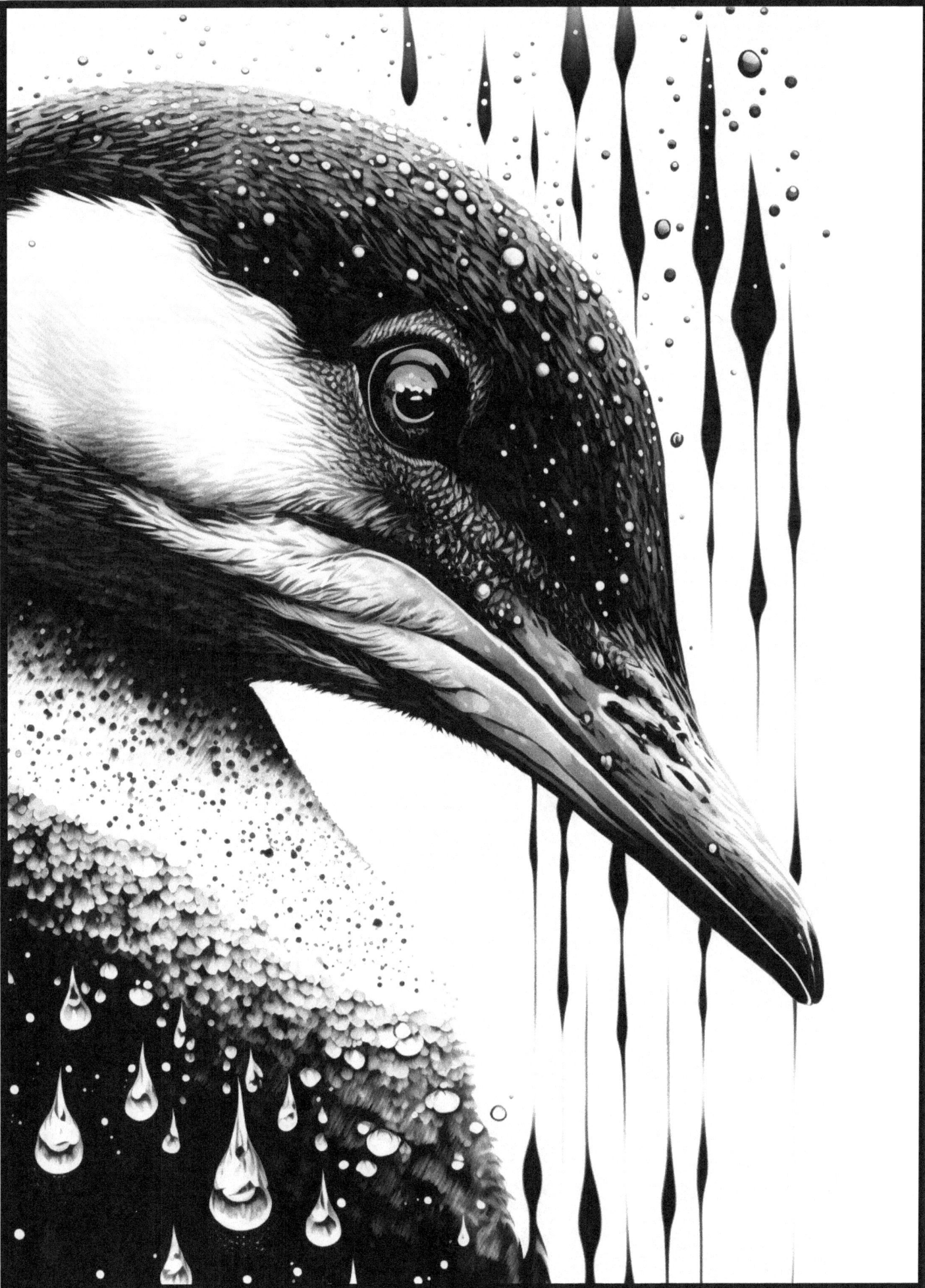

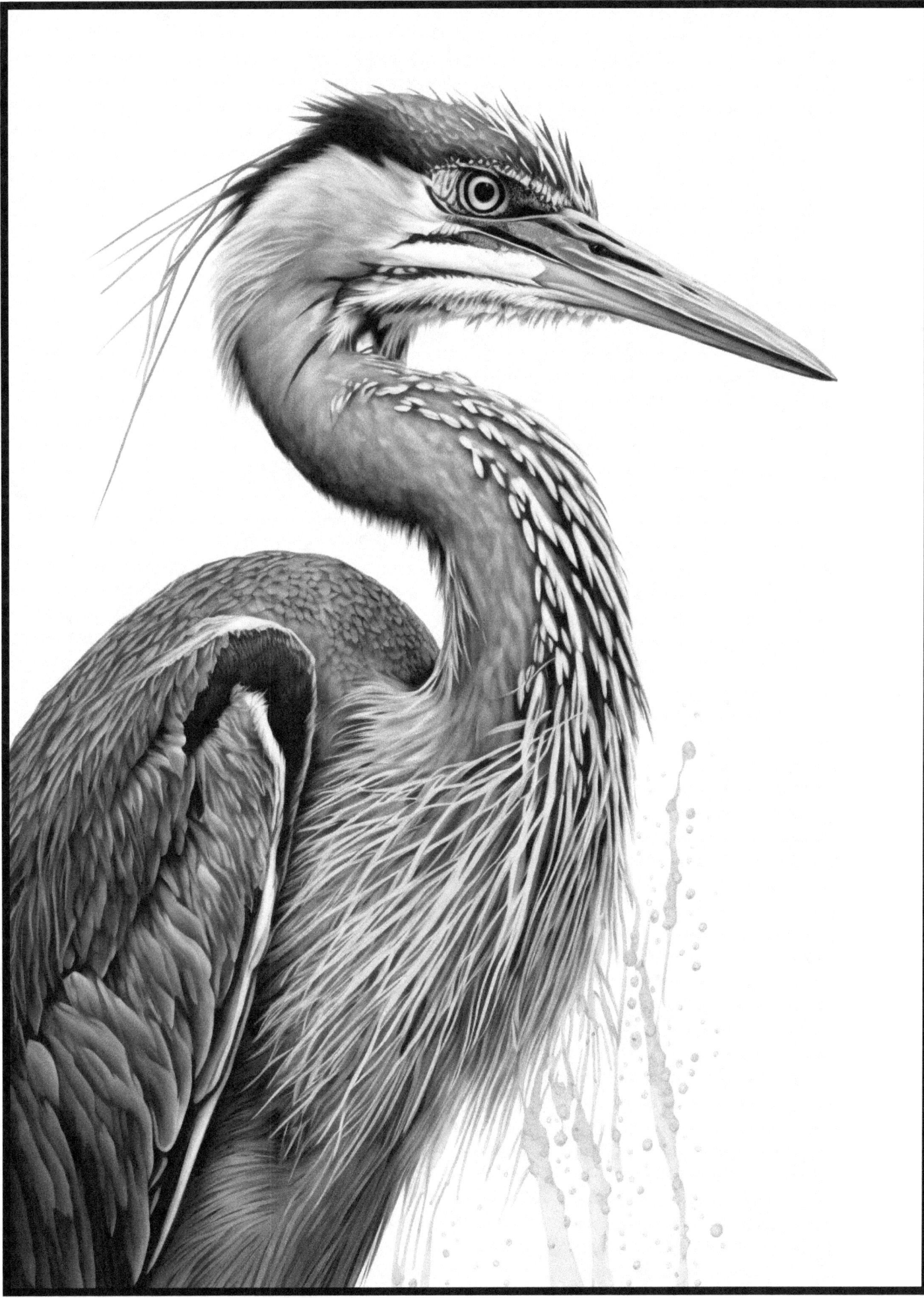

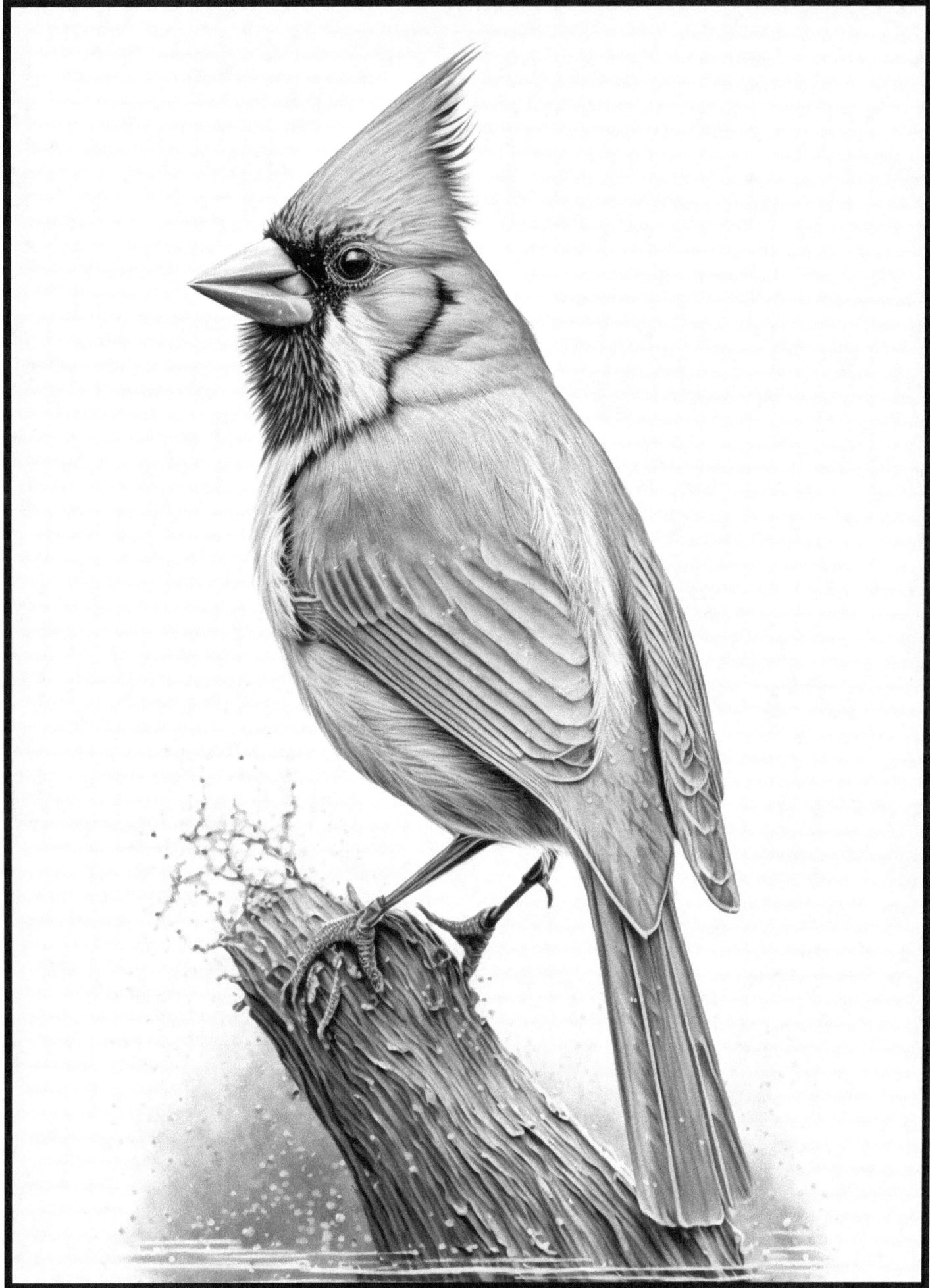

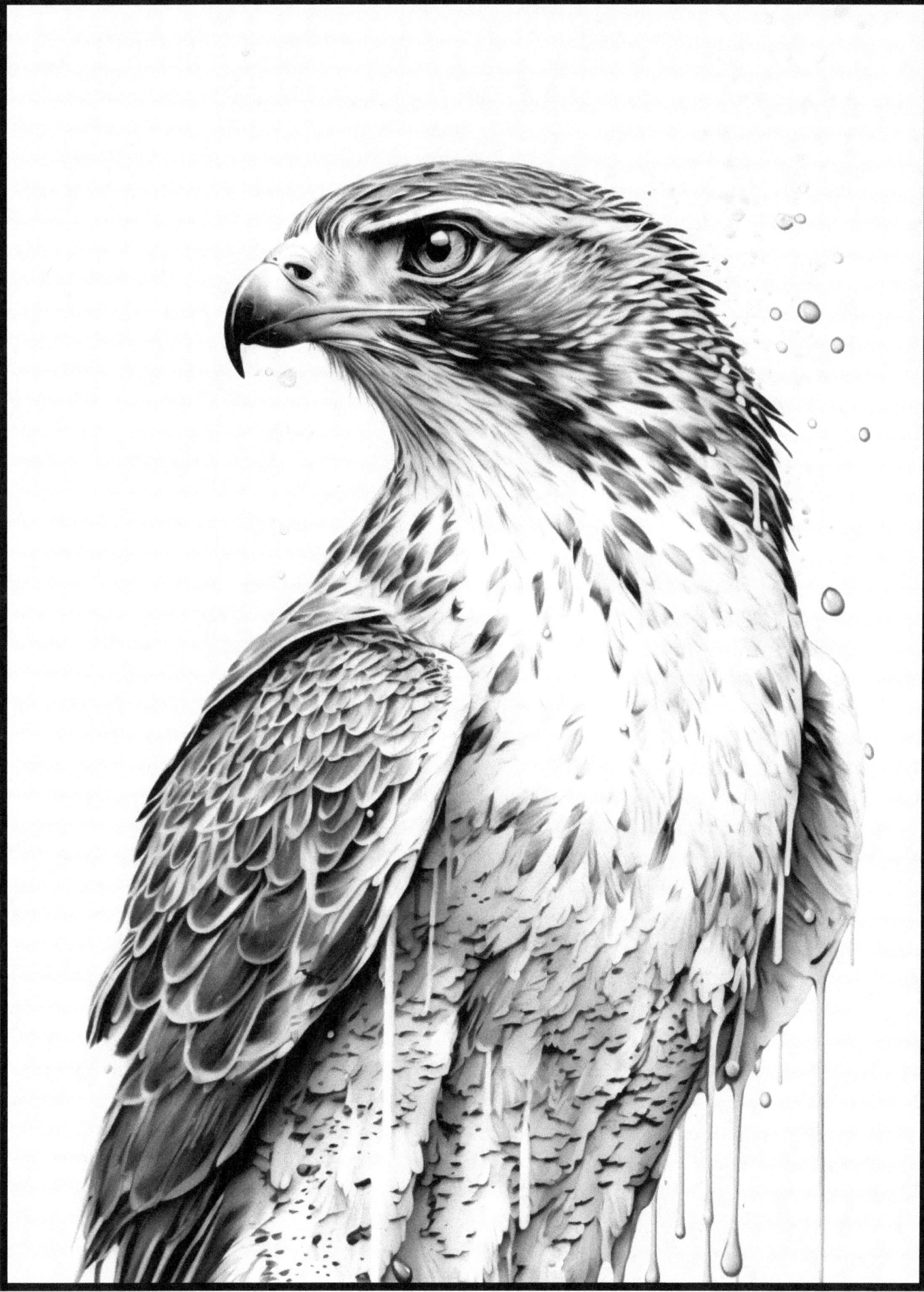

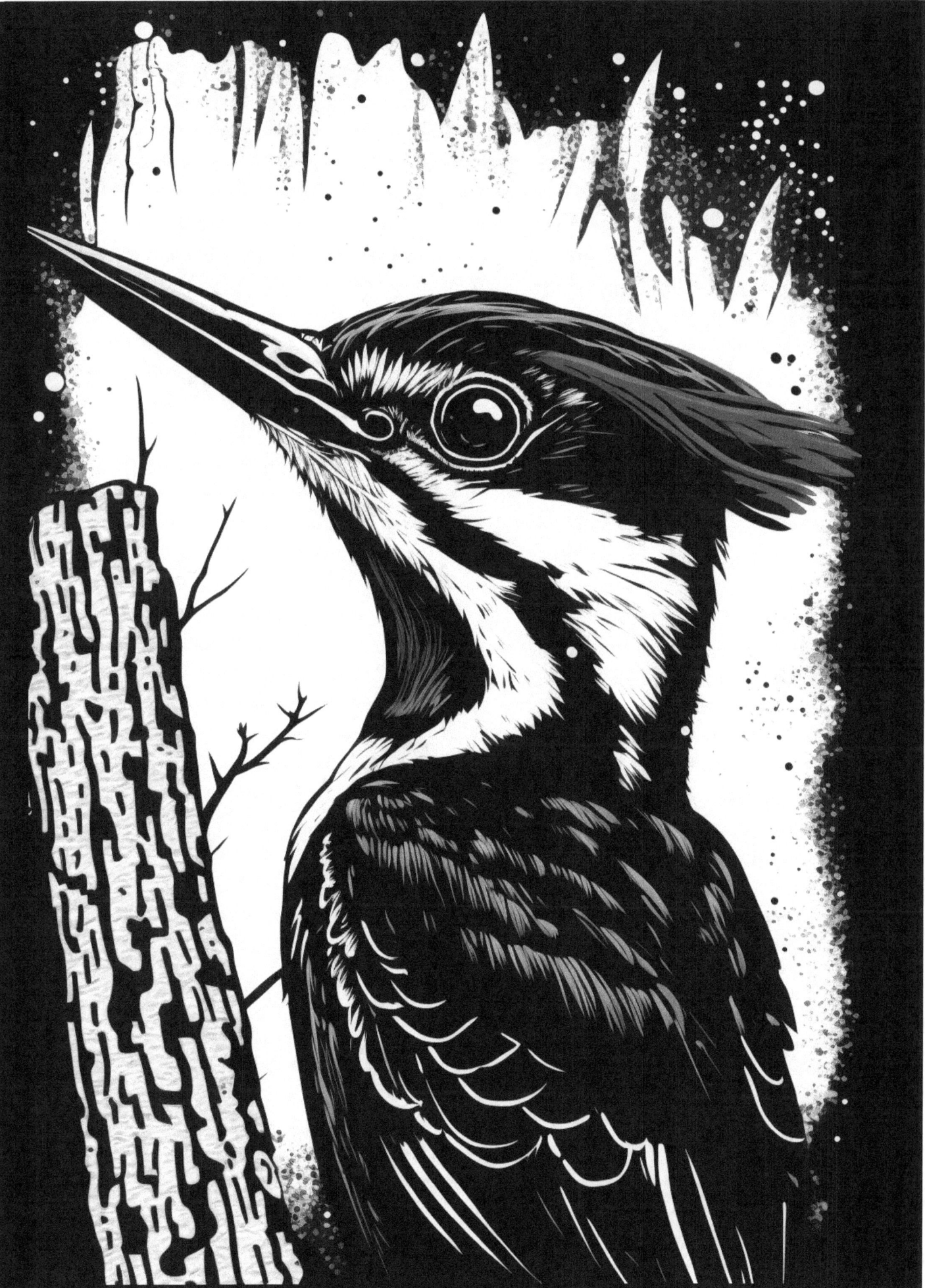

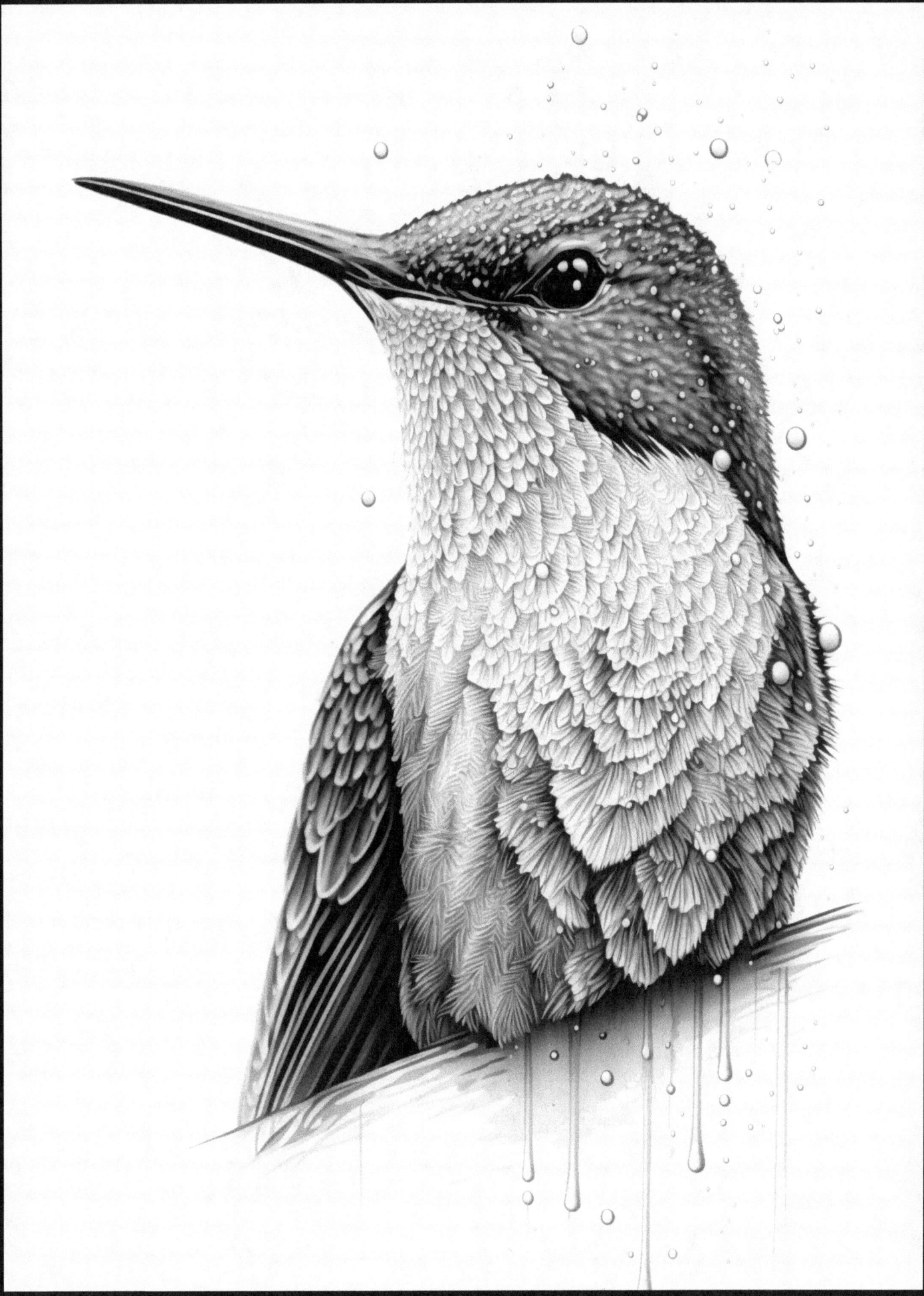

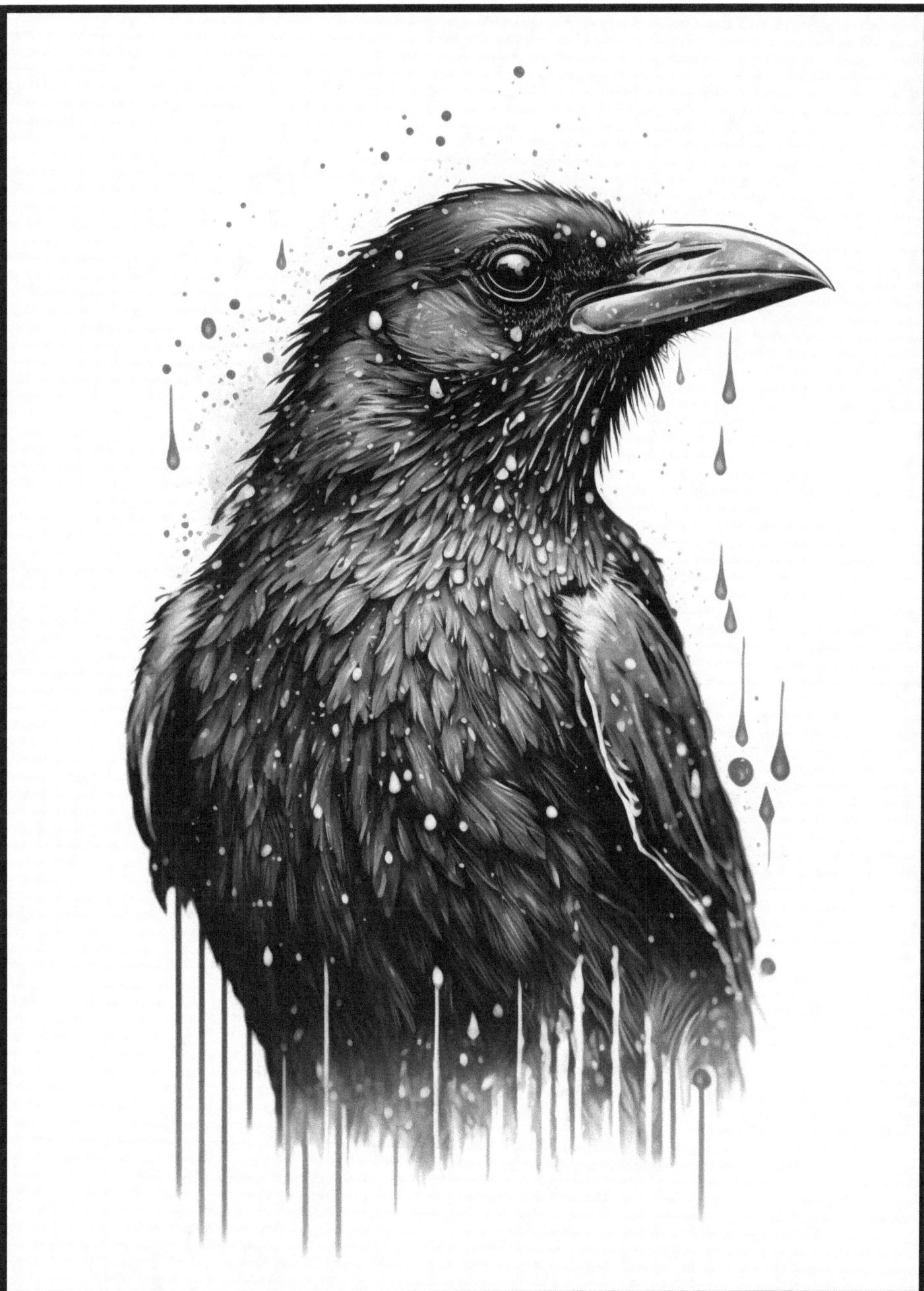

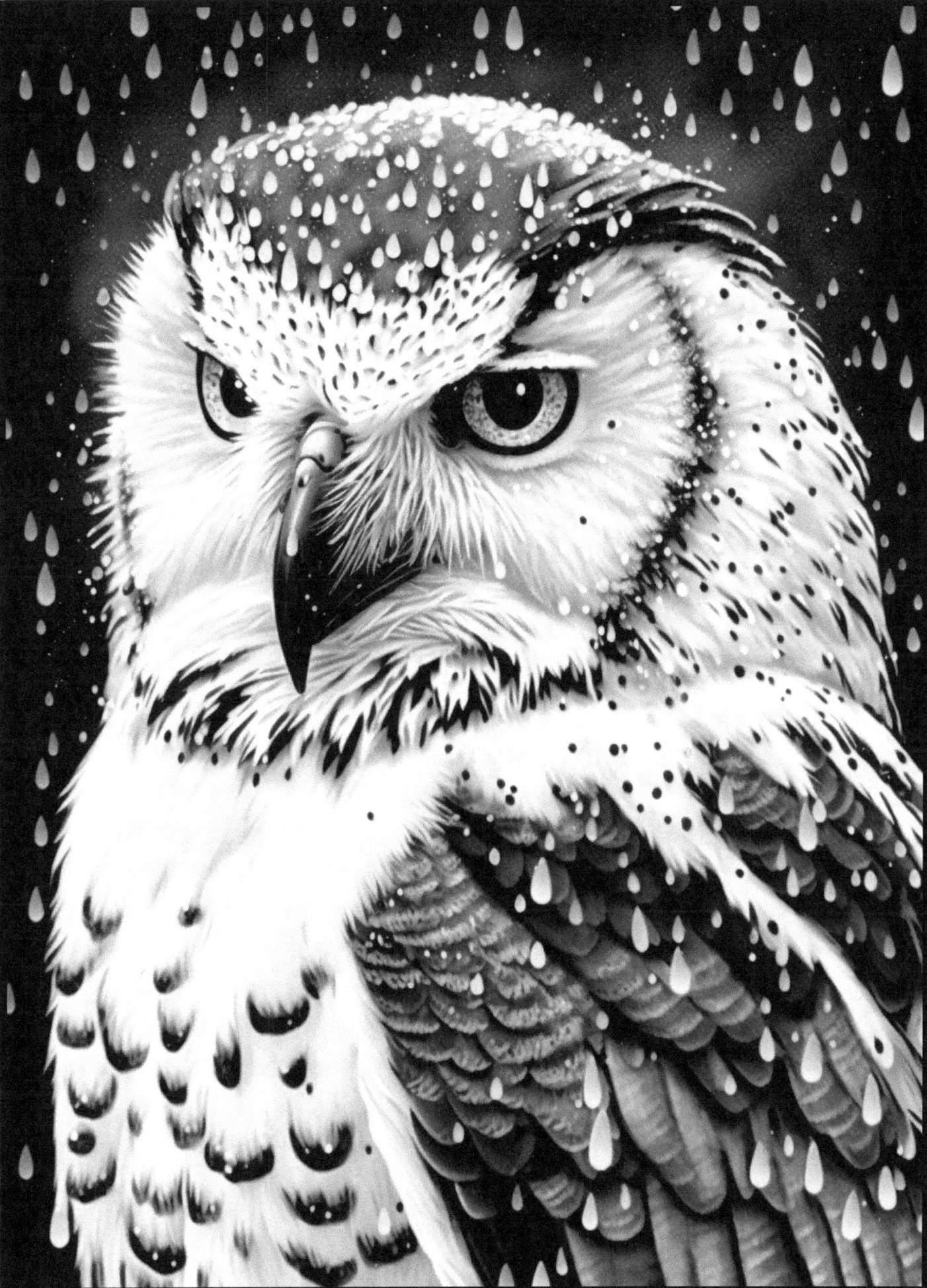

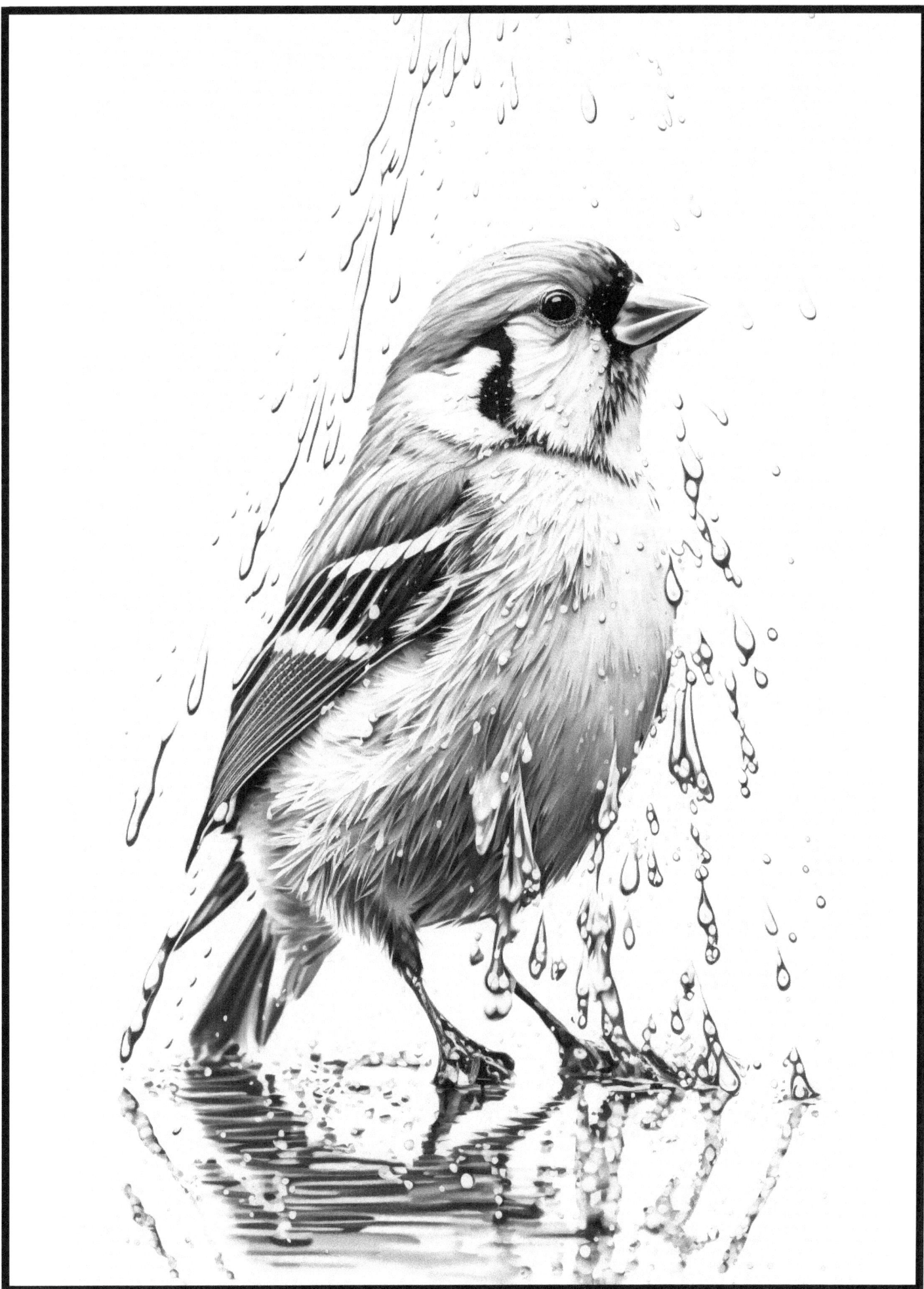

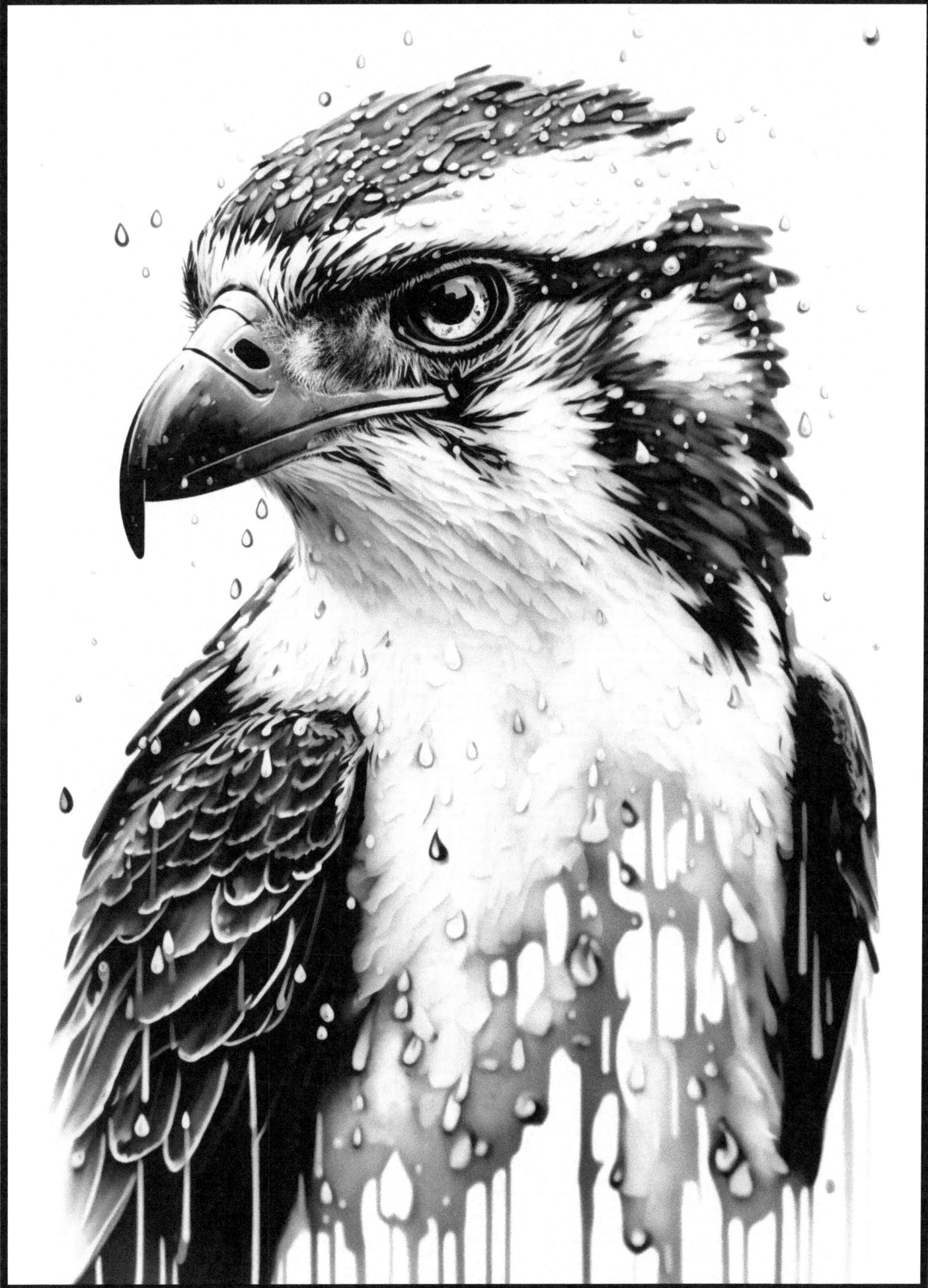

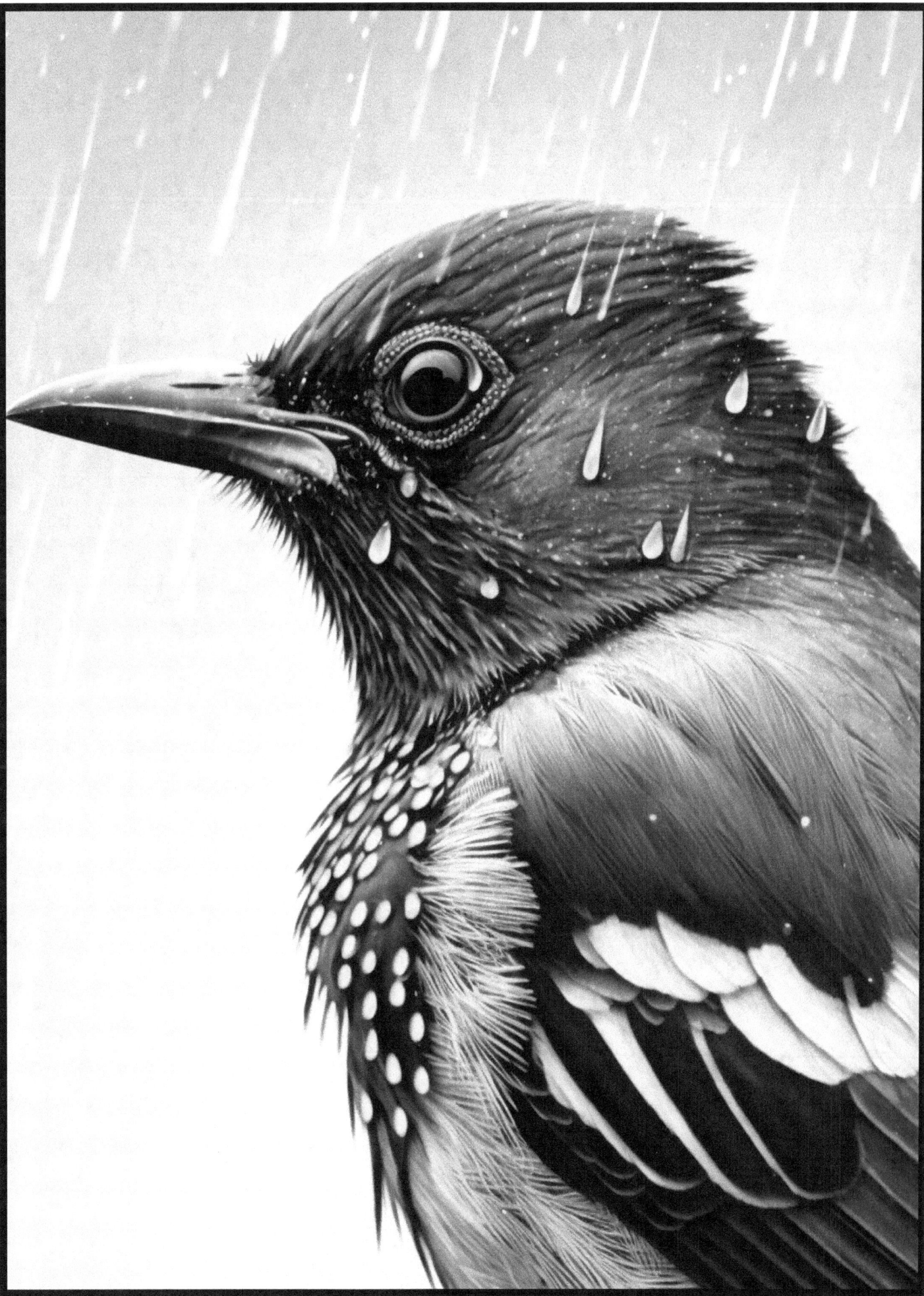

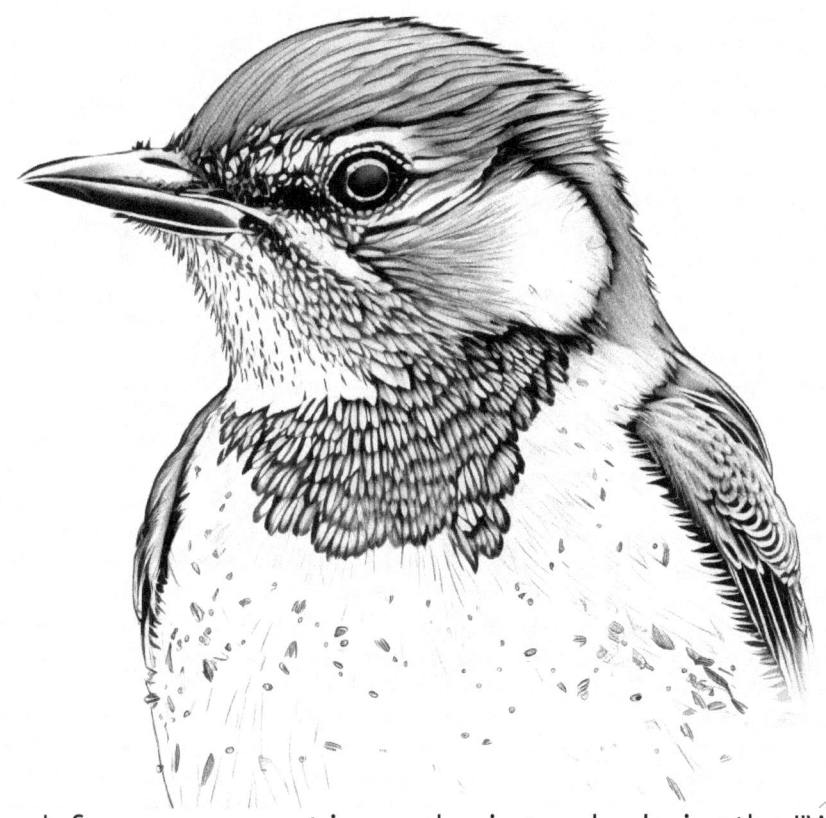

Thank you so much for your support in purchasing and coloring the "Wings of North America: A Coloring Book". Your encouragement and enthusiasm for this project means the world to me. I am thrilled to see that the book has helped you find moments of peace and relaxation. Your support has inspired me to continue creating art that brings joy and stress relief to people's lives.

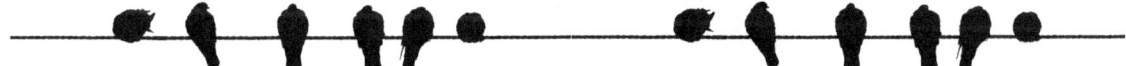